GG's Journey is a fictional account of a true story.

15% of net proceeds will be donated to animal rescue
to end animal homelessness, euthanasia of healthy and
treatable pets, exploitation, inhumane treatment
and animal cruelty.

Copyright © 2015 by Cheryl Lyn Phillips

Printed in the United States by
McNaughton & Gunn, Inc.

ISBN 978-0-9965109-0-5

ebook ISBN 978-0-9965109-1-2

Cover art and design: Deidre Stierle
&
Kim Hinman, Greko Printing Graphic Designer

Printed in the United States of America

2 3 4 5 6 7 8 9 / 16 17 18 19 20 21 22 23

IN LOVING MEMORY

Mary Rawa, My grandmother, and Bowser,
her faithful companion

My dad, who would be proud

The Borkowski Family

Carlton, Big Boy, Anthony, Lassie, Blobie and Diablo
Marshmallow and Ozzy

All of the animals that were never given a chance
to be loved

"The greatness of a nation and its moral progress can be judged by the way its animals are treated."

-Mahatma Gandhi

GG'S JOURNEY: FROM LOST TO LOVED

THE RESCUE

I remember every minute of that fateful day in May in the heart of Detroit. I sat in my usual spot on Maryland Street beneath the shade of a majestic oak tree. It was unusually hot, and the scorching sun glistened on the pavement. Very hungry and extremely thirsty, I was in bad shape. Although I didn't know my exact age, I think I was about two or three. I had been living on the streets of Detroit, eating scraps and taking shelter wherever I could. I never felt safe—I was always alone and on alert. Having survived in one of the city's oldest neighborhoods for many months now, I was still worried about my future. When you live alone on the streets, you become a good judge of character, and I was waiting for the right person to come along. I knew that it would take someone special to help me and that I had to time my cry for help perfectly. It was a matter of survival.

I'd lived with people once, but they hadn't been very kind to me. I slept under the porch in the back of their house, where it was too hot in the summer and biting cold in the winter. One fall evening, not long after I'd given birth to a litter of three puppies, the people moved away from the house and left us there. I was forced to look after my puppies by myself.

One terrible day, when I returned to the porch with scraps of food for my puppies to eat, I found them all gone. I didn't know what had happened—maybe the family had come back for my puppies but hadn't been able to find me. Maybe someone else, a stranger, had taken them away. I stayed at the house waiting for them to come back. After many weeks, I'd given up hope, so I left the house on my own to try my luck in the neighborhood.

Many other dogs in the neighborhood lived like I did. Though you might think that we would help each other out, I soon learned that not all of them were friendly as we were all trying to survive. Finding food and water on my own was very hard, and I knew that my only hope was to find another family to take me in.

The city of Detroit was changing. The neighborhood where I lived used to be full of families with children playing and pets chattering as you walked by, but now there was a thundering silence. People were moving out of the city to live in newer homes in the suburbs. Eventually, so many people left that there were thousands of abandoned homes resulting in increased crime and poverty for the people who remained. The houses on Maryland Street were no different than others on so many streets throughout Detroit.

Now living on my own I had noticed some more activity on the street. I heard rumors that they were trying to improve the neighborhoods. I'd watched dozens of volunteers come every week to build a new house down the street with a big sign in front of it that said "Habitat for Humanity." It was almost complete, and it looked much nicer than the other houses on the street, some of which had been abandoned and had tattered roofs, and broken and missing glass in their windows. That new house was a big change and I hoped it wouldn't be the only change—if more families moved back to the neighborhood, maybe one of them would have a new home for me, too. One of the few things that hadn't changed on Maryland Street was nature: beautiful oak trees lined the sidewalk, like the grand tree I claimed as my own. I imagined it had been there for hundreds of years and touched the sky.

As I sat under that tree watching the workers at the new house, something small and brown suddenly caught my attention across the street: a mouse! It darted into some large bushes, looking for food. Were there scraps of food for me there, too? With what little strength I had, I pulled all sixty pounds of myself up off the ground and padded across the street. Immediately I felt the scorching sun on my mostly white fur—some spots of fur on my coat had fallen out and on those patches the sun almost burned. But the prospect of food was worth leaving the comfortable shade of my oak tree.

I reached the bushes and began sniffing around. It was then I heard a loud "Shoo!" that made me stop in my tracks. Above the bushes, a woman was waving her arms at me from a first-floor window. Then a man appeared at the front door waving something long and metal in his hands. He began to walk down the porch steps towards me, and I immediately bared my teeth at him out of fear.

"Get out of here, pit bull!" he yelled.

I glanced longingly at the bushes and then retreated

to the oak tree. The woman watched me from the window with unkind, narrowed eyes. I lay down under the tree and rested my head on my paws, depressed and defeated.

Not far away, a lady walked to her car from the direction of the new house. She was slender, with dark hair and kind eyes. I had seen her on my street before. She wasn't scared of dogs like me—I'd even seen her stop and reach her hands out kindly to other dogs in the neighborhood who were out walking with their families. Today, as she walked across the gravel lot by my tree, she looked in my direction. Suddenly, I felt sure that this woman was my best chance to have a better life—or even just something to eat. I got up and walked slowly towards her. *Please don't be afraid of me, I thought. Please don't look away...*

She saw me. We both stopped. She didn't move; she didn't shoo me away like so many others had. I wanted to run up to her, but I didn't. I stayed very still to see what she would do next. After a minute or so, she turned away and walked quickly back to the house. My heart sank. I felt like I'd made a mistake. For the second time that afternoon, I settled under the tree again, feeling sad.

Five minutes passed. I lay my head on my paws and tried to nap. People think dogs just nap all day, but the truth is, it's hard to do. I didn't get very many hours of sleep living on Maryland Street because I always had to worry about surviving. I kept one eye open as I rested.

And that's how I saw her again—the kind-looking lady from the new house, walking toward me with part of a sandwich held in her hand. I jumped up, shocked. Was the food for me? I could hardly believe it!

"Come here, gal," the lady said. "Here you go."

As we moved toward one another, she put her hand out very slowly and gently. The lady laid the sandwich on the ground and watched to see what I would do. I padded forward and smelled it first—ham! I ate it so quickly, I can't even tell you how it tasted, only that it was the best food I'd had in a very long time.

"You were hungry, weren't you, gal?" said the nice lady.

I couldn't remember the last time someone had spoken kindly to me. I watched as she opened a bottle of water and poured it into a little red cup with ice cubes in it. It looked so cold and clean; I didn't just want to drink it; I wanted to swim in it! As I lapped it up, I felt it cooling my whole body. Suddenly, I felt overwhelmed. The excitement of eating and drinking made me feel exhausted and a little weak. I lay down on the gravel, wishing that there was some way I could tell this lady just how grateful I was. The scorching sun beat down on us both as the lady looked at me lying there.

"Get up and get back in the shade, gal," she said. Concern nipped at the edges of her voice. As she looked down at me, I saw that her forehead was furrowed with worry. "You'll only make yourself feel worse if you stay here in the hot sun." But I couldn't move. Instead, I let out a small whine. I hadn't wanted to sound as pitiful as I felt. I wanted to say thank you.

The woman frowned and went to her car. As she drove away, I felt my heart breaking. When would I ever find someone that kind again? When would I ever get to taste real food again or drink water that was clear and cold? My stomach growled at the thought of the sandwich I had just eaten. My mouth watered for more, but now wasn't the time to think about food. Instead, I watched a little bird hopping around on the grass. He was just a baby with black beady eyes and brown and white feathers on his wings. I wished that I could fly away from here. How badly I wanted to leave Maryland Street with the nice lady! She appeared, and then she'd gone, and I thought that my last chance for a better life had gone with her. But I was wrong again.

Not thirty minutes later, her car pulled into the driveway. She rushed over to me and opened a large bag, pulling out dog food, plates and treats. I couldn't believe my eyes. She poured a helping of dry nuggets and wet food into the bright new bowl—she wasn't going to let me eat off of the ground.

"That's right, you're a classy gal, aren't you?" she said softly.

The food was delicious! When she saw that I had eaten all of it, she gave me some more. After I had eaten for the second time, she slowly put her hand out to me. As I sniffed her, she knelt down and gently rubbed my head. Then she stood up and walked around the area. First, she waved at the man on the porch across the street, the one who had chased me away from his yard.

"Do you know if this dog belongs to a family?" she

asked him.

I wished I could speak to her, to tell her that my family was long gone and that a new one—a kind one—was my biggest wish. The man shook his head.

"Nope. Just another stray, that's my guess. Those dogs come around here all the time. Abandoned by their owners, I guess."

The lady thanked him and looked around for someone else to ask. She spoke to other people and pointed at me, but no one knew who my family was or how long I had been there. I wished I could tell her that I had once had a family. I don't remember much about who they were, but when they moved they hadn't taken me with them, and my beautiful puppies were gone.

Just then, a truck pulled up at the side of the road and a man got out. He waved to the lady and she said hello back.

"Cheryl, would you like to do the honors?" the man asked.

I was delighted to learn her name after she'd given me so much hope. It suited her personality and heart well, and I decided right then to refer to her as Aunt Cheryl. I watched as they talked for a while, then she moved towards me.

It was then that I realized what "the honors" meant: Cheryl carried a leash in her hand which she was trying to hide. I knew she was afraid that I would see it and run off. I didn't like leashes very much. My old owners had put me in a chain collar that hurt my neck when they pulled hard on it. As sick and exhausted as I was, I wanted her to see that I was a good gal who was gentle, sweet, and didn't cause any trouble. When she showed me the leash I just sniffed it.

She gently lowered the leash, placed it on me and led me over to where the man was waiting. He bent down and stroked my head.

"What a brave girl," he said. "You're not afraid, are you?"

I'll admit that I was a little bit frightened. I didn't know what was going to happen next, but I trusted the lady and knew that if she trusted him, I should too.

"She's very brave," Aunt Cheryl agreed. I looked up at her and was surprised to see tears in her eyes reflecting the sunlight. I imagined what I must have looked like to her: a street dog with a dirty, balding white coat and fleas. She saw my terrible hunger and thirst when I had lapped up the water and had eaten the sandwich in one gulp. I didn't want her to be sad. I barked softly to say *thank you, thank you for rescuing me.* Then the man lifted me into the back of the truck. He put me into a metal cage, and I became very nervous.

As he closed the van doors, Aunt Cheryl waved reassuringly at me and said, "I'll see you soon."

The truck was cool, and there was plenty of food and water for me. As I got used to the rumbling of the tires on the road, I relaxed a little and tried to sleep. But when the truck stopped, and the doors opened again, I was wide awake. The man lifted a huge dog inside, a Boxer with a short snout and sad, droopy eyes. The Boxer began to bark, and it echoed from the metal sides of the van. I sat up and circled my cage, wanting to get away. But once the man put him inside his cage and gave him some food and water, it put an end to his barking. He'd been hungry, just as I had been.

He looked at me, and though he didn't growl, he bared his teeth a little, as if to say, I need to be left alone. I'm scared, but not of you. I knew that he wasn't going to cause me any harm, but that he needed me to keep my distance.

The stops continued throughout the afternoon until there was a total of five of us. Although I was too tired to befriend these dogs, I've often wondered what happened to them. Two of them looked very similar to me and now when I think about them, I wish that I had asked these dogs if they'd experienced the same things I had. Had they been shooed away and yelled at more times than they could count because of how they looked? I didn't know this then, but I would soon learn so much about how people regard my breed—the kind of dog that I am—and that some people fear us.

But that afternoon, I wasn't thinking about any of that. Instead, I closed my eyes and tried to sleep, waiting patiently, hoping that the man would take me back to Aunt Cheryl. I had no idea what to expect. I was scared, but I was also excited to see what would happen next and relieved to have food in my belly and a place to sleep safely. My incredible journey was just beginning.

WEEK 1

Later that day, we arrived at an animal shelter. The man put me back on a leash and walked with me from the van into the building. As we entered, I smelled so many different dogs around me. I immediately became overwhelmed and scared. Those smells increased as the man brought me into a room lined with cages—in all of these cages sat other dogs. Many of them began to bark at me as I passed.

Although I wanted so much for the man to know that I was a good girl, I began to bark, too. I had met so many other dogs on the streets of Detroit and I'd learned to be cautious, but these dogs were not dangerous, just scared and lonely like me.

The man held my leash tightly and marched me over to a big cage out of sight of the other dogs. It was nicer than the cage on the truck and had a huge amount of food and water in addition to a big soft pillow. I walked into the cage and started eating the food, but suddenly everything went white. The man had put a sheet over my door. I didn't like this at all—I couldn't see anything! I barked and barked so the man would come back, but he didn't. Had I done something wrong? I was in a strange place, I wanted to see Aunt Cheryl, and I was frightened.

My stomach was bloated because of all the good food I'd eaten too quickly and I felt awful. I was very itchy and started to scratch myself. I lapped up some water. After a while, even though I hated that I couldn't see outside the cage with the sheet over it, I started to feel safe. I put my head on the pillow and tried to sleep.

As I drifted off, I tried to think of something nice to calm myself down. The nicest possible thing I'd ever heard of was Christmas. I hadn't known about this holiday until just last year. I had been wandering around the neighborhood one snowy December evening, searching for a place to keep warm when I passed a fenced-in yard with two dogs playing in it. One of the dogs, a mutt with short brown fur and a tear in one ear, came bounding over to the fence to say hello to me.

"Hey there!" she called, licking the falling snowflakes off of her pink nose. "Long time, no see!"

I stepped closer to the fence to get a better look at her. "I know you! Maggie, right?" I squealed.

"Yes, it's me," she replied, rubbing up against the fence to get as close to me as possible. Maggie had been a stray on the streets like me, hanging around over on Maryland Street most days. But then a few months back, she'd just disappeared. The thought had crossed my mind that she might have found a new home. But I had always feared the worst for her as cars, hunger, thirst and illness were constant threats to dogs living on the streets.

"You live here?" I asked as I looked beyond the fence at the clean, white house with lights glowing behind the curtains. I felt a twinge of pain in my heart for myself, but I was happy for her.

"Yes! I was adopted just a few months ago with this girl here," she said, nodding towards the other dog, a fluffy white thing with a brownish nose. "And the timing couldn't have been better!"

"What do you mean?" I asked.

"It's Christmas!" she said. "Don't you know what that is? My family has spent the past two months preparing for it," Maggie said, her tail wagging with excitement.

"It's a day when everyone gets extra love and presents and celebrates being part of a family. The people do all kinds of strange things to prepare for it—bring a tree into the house, decorate it with big shiny balls, and string bright lights everywhere. Everyone gets presents and good food on that day. Even us!" she said, nudging her new sister gently. "Shelly and I both got brand new bones, and squeaky toys—and we got to eat people food. It's been the best day!"

"It sounds perfect," I replied. But I couldn't help but feel my stomach growling and my paws shivering in the snow. Maggie suddenly looked very serious. "I wish you could join us," she said.

"That's ok, Maggie," I said, trying to sound hopeful.

"Maybe I'll have a Christmas with my very own family next year."

Since then, Christmas popped into my head every so often. I tried to imagine what it was like—my old family never spent a day celebrating Christmas when I was with them, or giving me extra food. I sometimes wondered if my puppies, wherever they were, knew about Christmas, or would ever experience it for themselves. I had many dreams during my time living on Maryland Street, and one of them was to have a family Christmas. I believed I would, I had to.

I had other dreams. I wanted someone who would scratch my head and play with me. I had visions of a safe home and snuggling in a warm bed. When I was so sick and weak that I could barely move, I would dream of long walks in the cool spring air, enjoying summer picnics in the park, and playing with children and tennis balls. In the fall, I wanted to watch from my bed as the red and gold leaves began to fall from the trees and float in the sunlight. On the winter streets, when I was so cold my paws were numb, I dreamt of sitting in front of a warm fireplace and watching snowflakes glisten underneath the moonlight. Any of these things, I thought, sounded like the special day called Christmas all by themselves.

∞

The next morning, I was in a wonderful mood. A hand came into the cage, took out the empty food and water bowls, and put in fresh ones. I started to eat, but then the hand lifted the sheet and light poured into the cage. I blinked and saw that the large room was filled with other dogs in cages. I remembered how afraid I'd been the day before and how I'd barked at them. I was sorry for that now. After a night of rest, it was easier to remember that these dogs were just like me, scared and hopeful all at the same time. I yipped cheerfully, just to say hello, and was happy to hear a cheerful bark or two echoed back at me.

The man who'd opened my cage wasn't the same

man from the day before. I felt uncomfortable having so many new people around me, but he smiled and took me gently by the collar. He put a leash on me, and I started to get a little excited. I was going outside!

He led me out the door and down a hall. Soon we were outside in a sunny patch of grass next to the shelter. The sun streamed over my body, warming me up. The man unclipped the leash and let me run. Fences on all sides of the yard let me know how far I could go. I walked slowly over the cool grass and found a tree in a far corner of the yard to rest under, it reminded me of my tree on Maryland Street.

Once there, I wondered whether I'd see Aunt Cheryl, again. I hoped so, very much.

I was enjoying the coolness of the shade and watching a pair of other dogs playfully wrestle when a lady entered the yard. I quickly bounded to my feet, and my heart started pounding. She turned toward me. I realized it wasn't Aunt Cheryl, and I was terribly disappointed.

This new lady, who was young and wearing a shirt with a paw print pattern on it, took me back to my cage and placed the sheet over it without saying a word. I didn't like the cage with the sheet. It was a dark, cold, and lonely place. I started to cry. I had woken up that morning feeling so rested and hopeful, but now I worried that nobody wanted me. Would I live alone in this cage with the white sheet and the hand coming to feed me for the rest of my life, I wondered. Although I was happy not to be on the streets, I hoped that my journey didn't end here.

I had several hours to myself in the cage that day, and I heard new animals enter the shelter. I could sense their relief to be off of the streets but also their fear of the future. A litter of tiny Labrador puppies became my neighbors that afternoon, and through a hiked-up fold in the sheet, I could see them in the cage next to me. They were very young, too small to be away from their mother, and their eyes were barely open. I wondered where their mother was and if, like me, she'd been doing her best to protect them before they were taken from her. Again, I thought of my lost babies. I had loved them so much; I missed them terribly. I hoped that they had found loving homes and were safe, but, unfortunately, the odds for them to find happiness were not great. I knew that before being taken to the shelter, but soon I got a nasty reminder of just how cruel the streets could be.

One night, a female dog was delivered to the shelter that looked very similar to me. Although people have often called me a pit bull, I am a mix of bulldog and terrier, and it turned out that she was a pure bulldog. That night, I heard her whimpering and pacing in her cage, across the aisle from me, for what seemed like hours. Some of the other dogs barked at her, as a sign to be quiet.

"What's your name?" I asked.

"Cleo," she said, in between whimpers.

"What's wrong, Cleo?" I finally gathered the courage to ask. She was keeping all of us from getting any sleep, and I just wanted to help.

"I miss my puppies," she cried. I immediately felt sorry for her.

"They were at the same house with me," she continued. "We were there to fight other dogs. I escaped, but they couldn't follow me. They get hurt all the time, but now I can't help and watch out for them!"

The other dogs grew quiet as she told her story. Her puppies, now almost fully grown, had gotten painful wounds on their chests and heads that would leave scars for the rest of their lives. I had never heard of anything like this.

"They have to fight other dogs?" I asked. "People make them fight? That's inhumane!"

The bulldog stopped pacing for a moment and looked at me with wide, wet eyes.

"You don't know?" Cleo said. "There are houses like that all over the country. I thought you would know better than anyone. Our breed is the one they like to make fight."

I was shocked. Was that why so many people on Maryland Street had chased me away? Was it because my breed was known to fight? But I wasn't a fighter. I couldn't believe what I was hearing.

I didn't sleep well at all that night. I kept waking up and peeking into the next cage to make sure that the five lab puppies were sleeping safely. I suddenly felt very protective of them. After hearing the story told by the bulldog, I was very worried about my puppies—had they been taken away and made to fight each other by some terrible, mean person? I hoped that these puppies wouldn't meet the same fate. They were now safe in the shelter, I hoped.

The next morning, I overheard a conversation that only confirmed what the bulldog had said. Two shelter employees came in to spray down the walls and floor of the room.

"I am very worried about Carolina," one worker said to the other.

"Why?" she asked.

"I don't know if she's going to be able to overcome her past. Whoever had her before I fostered her made her fight."

"Is she being aggressive towards you? Towards your other pets?" the co-worker asked. She sounded very serious and, as I listened, my fur began to bristle.

"She's not aggressive towards anybody in the house, but when she sees another bulldog mix, in the neighborhood, she barks, and I know it is out of fear. And, of course, every person that sees her do that thinks she's aggressive. She is a gentle and loving dog just trying to overcome her past. I won't give up on her. The rescued dogs from fighting rings are very misunderstood. The owners teach them to fight for their lives when all they want is love. It takes some time to gain their trust, but when you do they are loyal, loving, gentle companions."

"I don't know what to tell you," the co-worker responded, shaking her head. "Hopefully she just needs a little more time. Either way, though, that dog is lucky you took her in, because I don't think she would have been adopted otherwise. You know what would have happened to her then." She pointed to the door of another room at the end of the line of cages.

I didn't know what that room was for—but I knew that the other dogs, the ones who'd been here for a long time, were afraid of it. I had noticed in just my short time here that a couple of dogs had gone into the room and hadn't come back out. I shuddered to think of what was behind that door. And now these workers were talking about a dog who sounded very similar to me—if she might have ended up there, then what would be my fate? In the past, I'd needed to be cautious with other dogs—hopefully now I could leave that behind me. I was more determined than ever to show the shelter staff and Aunt Cheryl that I was a good girl who deserved a second chance.

∞

Three mornings later, a hand lifted the sheet from the cage, and I finally heard Aunt Cheryl's voice.

"Hello, Baby!"

I was so happy she hadn't abandoned me! I jumped up, stretched, and came right to the door, my tail happily wagging. She stroked my head with one hand and pulled out treats from her purse with the other. I lapped them up greedily. I wanted her to be the one to take me outside today. All I wanted to do was leave the cage and walk with her. I couldn't wait to feel her gentle touch on my head while the sun warmed my back and my feet touched the cool grass. But all of that would have to wait. Today she was just spending time with me inside and checking on my progress.

As she sat petting me, she suddenly broke into a smile. "You don't have a name yet. I think I'll call you Maryland," she said. I bumped my nose against the palm of her hand. I liked the name.

"Why Maryland?" asked a shelter worker in the room.

"It's the name of the street where I found her," said Aunt Cheryl, scratching behind my ears.

The other woman laughed. "It's a great name!" she said. "She looks like a Maryland."

Aunt Cheryl kept petting me, but her eyes suddenly became sad. She leaned in close to me.

"You're going to be ok, Maryland," she said, sighing. "I wish I could take you home myself, but I don't think my five kitties would get along too well with you!"

As she stood up, she dusted my fur off of her pants and stroked my head one last time.

"It's all going to be ok. We'll find you a wonderful home," she said. "I'll make sure of it."

When she came in again a few days later, I overheard her tell the shelter staff some good news. She'd set up something called the Maryland Fund, and it meant that other people like her would help me have a better life.

"She's going to have some medical bills while she's here," I heard her say to the young staff woman in the visiting room. "But I know we can raise the money needed to be sure she is taken care of."

The younger woman, whose shirt today had a fun pattern of colorful kitties, shook her head.

"I know, I wish we could afford to treat every animal

that comes in here the way they need," she said sadly. "Some of them just have so many health problems and there's not enough money. If only every one of our animals had a Maryland Fund!"

Aunt Cheryl looked at me sitting near her feet and smiled.

"Once she's healthy," she said, "I'm going to make sure that Maryland goes to a good foster home."

My heart thumped in my furry chest—a home! At that point, I didn't understand the difference between a foster home and a permanent home, but I so desperately wanted to realize my dream of finding a loving family. I was willing to do anything to help make it happen. For now, it meant being patient, being good, and healing. I was so happy to know that Aunt Cheryl wanted to help me fulfill my dream, even if she couldn't take me herself. My long and challenging journey had only barely begun.

∞

The next day, the shelter took photos of me to send to Aunt Cheryl so that she could show them to her friends from the Maryland Fund. The woman who'd laughed at my new name the day before put me on a leash. She led me to the visiting room, where she sat me down in front of the white wall and told me to stay.

But I was too excited! I couldn't sit still and the woman, whose name I still didn't know, had to hold my leash tightly while her coworker took the pictures. I'd never had my picture taken before and wasn't sure what to expect.

Flash!

The bright light frightened me, and I tried at first to wriggle away. The woman petted me, and I calmed down. *After all, I thought, this is what I have to do to find a family.*

As I was led back to my cage, I heard the woman talking at the front desk about the pictures. She and two coworkers were gathered around, looking at the back of the camera.

"These are great," the woman said. "Maryland looks much happier and more relaxed than when she arrived."

"Aw," said the younger woman with blonde hair. "She does, but I think she still looks a little sad."

As I settled back into my cage in the kennel room, listening to the muffled growls and shifting around of the other dogs, I had to agree with them. I was sad, and it didn't surprise me a bit that the feeling showed through in my pictures.

I was still a flea-ridden, sick, sixty-pound pit bull mix recovering from life on Maryland Street. Even worse, I was still upset about my puppies and angry that they had been taken from me before I'd had a chance to show them I could be a good mom.

"Hey there," said a kind voice. I looked up to see my new neighbor, the bulldog Cleo, looking at me with concern in her eyes. "You okay?"

I lay my chin down on my paws and exhaled.

"I'm not sure," I said. "I thought that getting picked up off the street would be the beginning of a new, exciting life. But I don't know what's going to happen to me. What if no one wants to give me a home after everything that Aunt Cheryl's done to help me? What if I'm just too sad, or too old, or too excited around other dogs?"

The bulldog lay down too, so we were at the same eye level. Many of the other dogs in the room went quiet as they listened.

"This is the beginning of something new and exciting, Maryland," Cleo said. "You can't help what happened to you in the past. You can only focus on being the dog you are right now. I've seen you around the people here. You're grateful and sweet, even if you do get a little nervous around some other dogs. So keep your chin up, ok? That's what I'm trying to do, for my puppies."

I nodded. Cleo was right. There was a lot to be scared of in the shelter, but I could take control of my fate by being a good girl, by being kind and calm. I'd keep trying and hope for the best. I was grateful to have Cleo to talk with, and she gave me hope. I was determined not to let my past ruin my plans for a second chance.

∞

A week had passed since my rescue and being taken to the shelter. The rule at this shelter was that no animal could be adopted until one week had passed, so that if we were lost our family could find us. Of course, I knew that no one would come for me from my old family. But Cleo, who had been in shelters before, told me that sometimes dog fighters—not the real family—come to shelters to try to adopt certain breeds of dogs for fighting. For that reason, she said that the shelter workers are very careful about who adopts the dogs, and for that matter cats and other animals. At the end of my first week in the shelter, I could rest a little bit easier. I didn't have a home yet. But at least I knew that I was completely safe from any human who might try to claim I was their pet and hurt and use me for the horrific, inhumane practice of dog fighting.

WEEK 2

On my eighth day in the shelter, I learned that I would be moved to a different shelter closer to Aunt Cheryl's home. I was excited that I would be closer to her but felt sad that I would have to leave Cleo and the Labrador puppies. I had become so attached to them. Before I could leave, I had another challenge to overcome: I had to be spayed so that I couldn't have any more puppies.

Naturally, this made me a little sad, especially when I thought about the puppies I'd had, whom I probably would never see again. But by being in the shelter, I had learned some things, and after seeing the large number of animals that came in every day, I knew that getting spayed was very important. I didn't want to bring more puppies into the world if there was no one to love and take care of them. If everyone who had a pet acted responsibly and spayed and neutered their pet, and shelters did not adopt out pets until they were spayed or neutered, we could save tens of thousands of lives. Also, the shelters would not be full of homeless and neglected animals. I thought how wonderful that would be. Each day I saw far too many dogs like me, and cats, too, that were subject to homelessness, abuse, and neglect. I could only hope that I would be one of the fortunate ones who would find a loving home.

After I had been spayed, I was ready to be moved from Detroit to a shelter in the suburbs. The cheerful man who had helped Cheryl with me that first day on

Maryland Street loaded me into a cage in his truck, and we were off. As the truck jostled along the city roads, I became very uncomfortable, still sore from my surgery. When we finally reached the shelter, I felt woozy and tired. The faces of the workers at the new shelter loomed above me, talking to me, but I felt too dizzy to greet them.

"Someone's in need of a little rest," said the man, and he escorted me to my new, clean cage in the suburban shelter. The room with the cages was a crisp white with a window out to a yard where some other dogs were playing. I wanted to join them, but not until I'd had a nice long nap. I spent most of that day resting and drinking water.

Later that evening, though, my restful day was interrupted in the worst possible way. One of the handlers, an older woman with curly brown hair, came in to take me outside before shutting me in my cage for the night. I was still groggy and didn't feel very well.

As she led me down the white hallway to the outside yard, I heard the main door of the shelter open and the barking of a large, frightened dog. It was a large German shepherd entering the shelter for the first time pulling at his leash. I remembered seeing German shepherds back in the old neighborhood, but they weren't like the homeless dogs—they were always with men and women in blue uniforms who drove white cars with flashing lights and wailing noises. They were confident dogs and I wondered why he was here. As my walker and I drew closer, the German shepherd's eyes focused on me. I saw the desperate, scared look in his eyes. I knew he was about to start barking at me and I felt the pangs of fear that had become so familiar to me during my time on the streets.

My walker and I were closing in on him and, with no way for us to avoid each other, I suddenly jumped up on my hind legs and began barking at him. He barked back. My walker immediately pulled me away from him.

"Bad girl! Maryland, shame on you! You should never jump at another dog, ever."

As I watched the other handler pull the German shepherd away, whimpering, I felt ashamed. I should have remembered that he was only acting so upset because he was scared, too. I'd had a long day, and I'd forgotten what I'd learned from Cleo—that I was the one in control of my fate, and that if I was going to find a home, I had to remember to be as patient with other dogs as Aunt Cheryl and the shelter workers were being with me.

The next day, I was so excited to hear my favorite voice when I woke up:

"Hi Maryland, how are you today?"

Aunt Cheryl had come to visit and brought me chewy treats and bones. Somehow she knew exactly what kind of treats I loved.

"You look like a new dog, Maryland!" Aunt Cheryl said. Today I did feel like a new dog for the first time since my rescue. I hoped that no one would tell her how badly I'd acted the day before. I wanted, more than anything, for my time at this new shelter to be a fresh start.

She put a leash on me and took me out to the bright, green yard. I loved being outside, feeling the soft grass on my feet and the cool breeze on my skin. It was hard to believe that a few weeks earlier I had been so exhausted and sick that I couldn't even enjoy my surroundings.

A couple of other dogs were outside with their handlers, too, but I was relieved to see that the German shepherd wasn't there. I pulled at the leash, eager to play and to show that I could get along. One of the handlers, though, was the woman who'd taken me out the night before. She looked at me with narrowed eyes, as though she thought I was about to jump again.

"Maryland seems much more playful now that she's feeling better," Cheryl said to the woman. She walked over to her, and I was careful not to bark or jump at the dog the woman was walking, a handsome, scruffy mutt with gray, curly fur.

"Hi there," I said to the mutt. "It's a great day, isn't it?"

"I guess," said the mutt, who seemed more interested in digging at some dirt by the fence than talking to me. I shrugged it off and went to sit next to Aunt Cheryl's feet.

"She's doing much better than when I first found her over a week ago," Cheryl was saying to the woman. "She's interacting more," said the woman. "And she looks so much healthier than she did in those pictures you took for the Maryland Fund, but…" The woman trailed off.

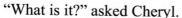
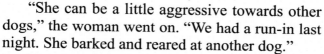

"What is it?" asked Cheryl.

"She can be a little aggressive towards other dogs," the woman went on. "We had a run-in last night. She barked and reared at another dog."

I hunkered down on the ground, ashamed. If only I had a voice, I could have told Aunt Cheryl that I wasn't trying to be bad; I was only scared. Now that I knew the staff was holding this incident against me, I felt a bit depressed.

Cheryl leaned down and scratched behind my left ear. "I don't see anything in her behavior today that worries me," she said. I looked up and thumped my tail against the ground. I should have known that Aunt Cheryl wouldn't hold one little bark and jump against me! "Look at her now—she's fine out here, with other dogs. She just needs a little time to get used to being safe," she said.

I was so happy that Aunt Cheryl was pleased with my progress. I knew she would not give up on me. After all, I had been doing my part by making friends with the shelter staff and in return many of them were working to ensure that I had a second chance. As our time that day came to an end, we returned inside. She kissed me on the forehead and promised to return next week. I had never experienced such love, trust, and compassion. Her voice now was ingrained into my mind and I realized that if she believed in me and my dreams, then I had to, too.

As the woman with curly brown hair led me back to my cage, she smiled at me.

"That woman is doing so much to find Maryland

a home," she said to the attendant in the kennel room. "I think we must have a pretty special dog on our hands." I felt a warm buzz of pride all over my fur. If I could win this woman over, then I could do anything.

∞

A few nights later, I was trying to fall asleep when I felt a small paw touch my side.

"Psst," said a quiet voice.

"Who's there?" I replied, lifting my head up off of my paws, suddenly alarmed and alert.

The voice belonged to a tiny Chihuahua in the cage next to me.

"Relax," the Chihuahua laughed. "I'm just your friendly neighbor. I'm not here to hurt you. My name is Bunnie. Funny name for a dog, eh?"

"Hi, I'm Maryland. Just a natural reflex, I guess," I said. "In my old neighborhood, getting woken up by another dog usually meant danger."

"You don't have to tell me about that," the Chihuahua said. "I bet I've spent more time on the streets than any dog in this place."

I found that a bit hard to believe—this tiny dog looked like she could have been a puppy!

"Do you know how old you are?" I asked.

The Chihuahua shook her ears proudly. "I am at least seventy in people years."

"Wow," I said, laughing. "I'm not sure I've ever met a dog as old as you."

"Trust me; this age has come at a price," Bunnie said.

"Though, of course, I'm very happy to be alive."

In the pale moonlight shining through the window, I could just make out what looked like a tired smile.

"What was the price?" I asked.

She scooted up against the bars of her cage to get as close to me as possible.

"The price, my dear, was my freedom for quite some time." She paused and then sighed. "Unfortunately, humans control this world and they certainly control animals' destinies. My family didn't feed me. They wouldn't walk me. I hardly remember a day for the first five years of my life when I wasn't thirsty. When I would cry for food or water, they would beat me as if it were my fault…" She trailed off.

I was stunned. I had experienced lots of pain, but I was never beaten.

"Well, the most important thing is that you are safe now," I said, not sure of what else I could say. "No one can hurt you here."

"I certainly hope you're right," Bunnie replied, curling herself into a tiny ball for the night.

It wasn't the first time—and certainly wouldn't be the last—that I settled back to sleep feeling grateful that I'd been lucky enough to avoid many of the horrors that some animals faced every day. My last thought, before I fell asleep, was that one day, I wanted to find a way to help them, the way Aunt Cheryl had helped me.

WEEK 3

When I wasn't sleeping, eating, or drinking in my cage, I was talking to my new neighbor friend. Bunnie had a fiery personality, and because of what she'd been through, she didn't trust the staff members very much. But we became good friends, and I hoped that I could have a calming effect on her. I also needed someone to talk to as I tried to process all that was happening to me. One day, I told her what had been weighing most heavily on my mind since being taken off the streets.

"In some ways, it has been so hard to be here," I said to her as we lay side by side in our cages. "I'm certainly thankful for the roof over my head, the food, and the attention, but my emotional wounds seem to be getting worse, not better."

"Is there a particular reason?" she asked.

"In the last shelter, there was a litter of puppies that slept next to me," I said. "And they made me remember some things I'd tried to forget from my many months on the street. I used to have some puppies of my own," I told her. "But I don't know what happened to them. I've always hoped they were safe, but now I know about dog fighting... I don't know if those little lab puppies at the last shelter ever found a good home, and I don't know what happened to mine, either. I couldn't help them..." I trailed off. The tiny Chihuahua looked teary-eyed for a moment.

"Maryland, nothing is ever going to erase the pain of losing your pups, but you have wonderful memories of them. I know this may not be what you want to hear right now, but you can't beat yourself up for something you had no control over."

I sighed deeply. "And just how do I do that?"

Bunnie smiled. "Maryland, just look at the bright future you have ahead of you. You have a wonderful woman who cares about you more than I've ever seen anyone care about an animal before. Imagine what the two of you will do together once you get out of this place!"

"She is amazing, isn't she?" I laughed. "Who would have ever looked at me, the way I was on Maryland Street, and told me I was a classy gal!"

"That's right," said the Chihuahua. "And because of her love, you are a classy gal! If you ever feel that you have to tell yourself a story about what might have happened to your puppies, imagine that each one of them met their own Aunt Cheryl."

I was in good spirits after this conversation and had a renewed sense of hope and purpose. Little did I know what was to come…

∞

A few days passed and I was gradually becoming sore, weak and dizzy. One morning I felt something warm near my belly and when I looked to see what it was, I was shocked. Red liquid was beginning to trickle out of me into my cage. I panicked and started barking.

"Help!" I called, over and over, but the shelter staff had not arrived yet. No one came and opened the door to the kennel room.

The other dogs in the room, including my friend Bunnie, began rustling in their cages and craning their necks to see what caused my distress. I could hear their voices.

"What's going on?"

"What's wrong?"

"Cut it out!"

"Oh no! Maryland!" shouted Bunnie, who began barking too.

By the time the first staff member opened the door that morning, the entire kennel was in an uproar, and I was too exhausted to yelp for help anymore.

The staff member, a young man who wasn't as thorough as the more experienced staff, went around to all the cages to refill food and water bowls.

"Quiet down," he said. He did his best to drown out my neighbors' yips and howls by wearing his headphones. When he finally did open my cage to give me food and water, I was too weak to show him that something was wrong. My body covered all of the blood in the cage. He closed the door after leaving the food, and he left the room.

"Come back here, you…you….grrrrr!" My Chihuahua friend was upset to see that I hadn't gotten help. As for me, I could only lay on my cage floor in pain.

Thankfully, Aunt Cheryl came to visit me not long after the shelter opened, but I was so weak I couldn't even stand up to greet her. It didn't take her long to discover something was very wrong. I watched as her radiant smile melted and was replaced by confusion and horror. With a ghostly-white face, she rushed over to the shelter staff and begged them to help me. Although I knew she had gone to get help, I was anxious and felt very alone. I could feel the wetness start to pool under my fur. I didn't know what was happening, or if I would receive the help I so desperately needed in time. With what little strength I could muster, I began to whimper.

Finally, a veterinarian approached and carried me from my cage into a medical room where another man gave me a shot. I fell asleep almost immediately. When I woke up, Aunt Cheryl was by my side gently petting me and looking into my eyes. The color had returned to her face, and she seemed much less terrified than she had been earlier. The veterinarian stood across the room, telling her what he'd found out.

"Maryland suffers from a very rare and very deadly infection called peritonitis, but luckily we caught it in time to treat it," he told Cheryl. "We'll need to keep her in the veterinary wing, hooked up to a tube that will give her the amount of medicine she needs to fight the infection."

Although I was still scared and worried that the tube and the medicine would hurt me, Aunt Cheryl's presence gave me a sense of relief. I was hooked up to the tube that gave me the medication I needed, and one of the staff members returned to take my temperature several times that day. Although I felt terrible, I was determined to survive.

WEEK 4

When Aunt Cheryl came to visit me a few days later, my temperature was still being taken several times a day, and I was receiving regular shots of medication. I was recovering from my surgery, and I had on a huge plastic collar. At first I didn't understand why I had the collar (called an Elizabethan collar or pet cone). I learned later that it was for my own good because otherwise I would have licked my stitches. After everything I'd been through, I was more thrilled than usual to see Aunt Cheryl—she had saved my life again! I greeted her with a wet, warm kiss and a tail wag while she fussed over me.

"Maryland's recovering very well," the veterinarian told Cheryl. "But I hear from some other staff members that she can get a little too excitable around the other dogs. We're trying to keep a close eye on her."

I was so frustrated upon hearing this that I immediately turned to Bunnie.

"Hello friend," I said as soon as I re-entered my cage after a brief walk outside. "I don't mean to bother you, but I really need to vent!"

"Sure," she said, lifting her warm eyes to face mine. "What's wrong?"

"I don't think the humans here understand me at all," I sighed.

"Why do you say that?" she asked.

"I've been trying so hard to be friendly with the other dogs. I try to play with them, instead of barking and jumping. Clearly, though, dogs like me are not allowed to make a single peep; otherwise we're put on the bad list."

"Oh, yes, I've noticed that they seem to have a double standard when it comes to certain types of dogs," she said. "Now, if I were to start barking they would not pay much attention. If you were to do the same, they would accuse you of being aggressive. I understand, dear. I know it's frustrating."

"That's an understatement," I sighed.

"I know it's unfair," Bunnie continued. "But just like with your puppies, you can't be angry forever. If there is one kernel of knowledge you take away from me, I hope it is this: You and I are only one generation. You and I will suffer because people are too quick to judge, but that does not mean that the next generation must. You will go on to do wonderful things and show the world what pit bull mixes and shelter animals are about. We are all wonderful animals looking for loving homes."

What the shelter staff didn't seem to understand was that before entering the shelter I'd never had an opportunity to play with other four-legged creatures. When I lived in Detroit, I knew other dogs, but I never had a chance to play with them or to enjoy friendships with them. At times, we would curl up together to stay warm on freezing Michigan winter nights. Sometimes we would ban together to claim territory and prevent other animals from competing with us for food, water, and shelter. However, when resources were extremely scarce, we competed for the last bit of garbage or the last drop of water since it could have been the difference between life and death. For homeless dogs, the highest priority is survival. When you have spent your entire life on the streets and are rescued and taken to a shelter, it is difficult to know how to behave.

A dog with my history needed patience, understanding and human love. Given the additional struggles I was facing lately, I desperately wanted the shelter employees to see me as kind, loving and smart like Aunt Cheryl did. Living in the shelter was quite stressful for me, and for all of the animals. No one seemed to consider how different my behavior would be if I were in a loving home. How I wished that I could go back in time and prevent myself from barking and jumping at the German shepherd! Unfortunately, if the staff believed I was aggressive, they might not be able to find me a foster home. I was beginning to understand how the stereotypes associated with my breed could negatively impact my future, and I was more determined than ever to prove that I was adoptable.

I didn't have a voice to express this, so I depended on Aunt Cheryl to challenge the stereotypes that were now threatening my dream of finding a loving family. She knew that I was not aggressive and refused to let the shelter staff believe it. I'll never forget how she looked at the veterinarian after he updated her on my condition that day.

"Maryland has come so far already," she'd said to him. "I believe in her—and I believe that she's a sweet, good girl. If some of the staff here might be letting their preconceived ideas about pit bull mixes stop them from getting to know her, just wait—she'll prove them wrong."

One of the many lessons I learned on my journey was that sometimes it only takes one person advocating for you to make a difference. I would never have believed that in my darkest, most desperate hour, this wonderful woman would appear and change my entire life. I learned the importance of keeping my dreams alive and never giving up hope, even though so many others had turned their backs on me before. Despite the persistent belief that I was aggressive and not adoptable, Aunt Cheryl continued to have faith in me and never stopped working on my behalf. If it were not for her love, compassion and patience, my fate would have been drastically different.

I was fortunate to have a guardian angel. Tragically, many other animals in the shelter were not as lucky as me.

WEEK 5

Aunt Cheryl continued working very hard with the shelter, her friends and a local pit bull advocacy group to raise money for my medical bills and find me a foster home. After five weeks, her efforts started to pay off. One of her good friends, a lifetime dog-lover, Anne, expressed interest in fostering me. As a foster mom, Anne would keep me for a short time until I was adopted so that I wouldn't have to live at the shelter. Aunt Cheryl was very anxious to find a foster home for me because I was still recovering from multiple medical conditions and required special care. However, Anne already had two dogs, so she asked the shelter director for an assessment of my behavior before making her decision. Aunt Cheryl shared the shelter director's report with Anne. Unfortunately, it gave mixed results:

Dear Cheryl,

I was told you had a nice time walking Maryland and that she was able to get lots of sun and fresh air while you were with her. She is doing pretty well, and we are confident that we can find a home for her. We just need to determine what the best course of action would be in her case and then commit the financial resources to get us where we need to be with her. She has some medical issues that we need to address relating to the itchiness that she has experienced since her rescue. She also seems a bit depressed and needs to get out of the shelter environment.

We cannot guarantee her health if you decide to

foster her. We may be dealing with long-term health issues that may or may not be contagious to other dogs. Her behavior was all right, but she seemed to have an issue with a male dog we introduced her to. She rose up on her hind legs, growled, and challenged him. She is a bit unpredictable and, again, we cannot guarantee that Maryland will not have issues with other dogs. If you want a promise that there won't be any issues, we can rule you out as a potential foster parent.

Aunt Cheryl visited the next day and shared this news with me: Anne was concerned that I was "unpredictable," and she worried about me being around the two dogs she already owned.

"I'm disappointed," Aunt Cheryl said to the woman at the shelter as she scratched my ears. "But something wonderful will turn up." As for me, I was disappointed, too. I had spent over a month in the shelter now and had seen dozens of dogs, kittens, ferrets and rabbits find foster and permanent homes. Would I ever experience what so many other rescue animals had? Although this was certainly a setback for me, I knew that I couldn't give up. I just needed an opportunity to show potential foster parents what a good girl I was. Aunt Cheryl already believed in me, and I knew that she was working harder than ever to give me that opportunity. For now, I just had to be patient and continue to hope.

A few days later, Aunt Cheryl visited again, with better news. She had been at a meeting about proper animal treatment (Humane Education) and began telling my story. Another person told Aunt Cheryl that she needed to meet Grace, an animal lover who had fostered dozens of dogs like me. In addition to her foster commitment, she owned a doggie day care, volunteered hundreds of hours at an animal shelter, and did legal work on behalf of voiceless animals. Aunt Cheryl was overjoyed that she had found this amazing and passionate potential foster parent and sent Grace my story and photos.

"And guess what? She wrote back almost immediately!" Cheryl told me. "Grace said you're a beautiful girl—you even look a lot like one of her current dogs Ozzy."

"Someone's adopting Maryland?" the woman at the shelter asked as she saw Aunt Cheryl petting me in the hallway.

"We're not quite there yet," Aunt Cheryl told her. "But we may have a foster home for her! Grace wants to meet Maryland right away."

"Congratulations, Maryland!" the woman said, walking away.

Aunt Cheryl bent down and tousled my ears a bit. "Once Grace read your story, she agreed that you should get out of here as soon as possible," she said. "You deserve a home where you can be looked after like the wonderful gal you are!"

When I returned to my cage after hearing this news I was grinning from ear to ear.

"What is it?" my neighbor Bunnie asked. "I know something big happened."

"Is it that obvious?"

"Oh yes," she laughed.

"There's a lady that's interested in fostering me," I said. Just saying those words was exciting, my tail started wagging before I even knew it. "She's coming to visit me next week. She works with dogs like me all the time, and she loves helping us."

"Aw, Maryland," Bunnie said. She reached her paw through the bars of the two cages to touch my shoulder. "I am so incredibly happy for you. You deserve it."

"Don't you think you deserve it more, Bunnie?" I asked, suddenly feeling a bit guilty. My friend had seen so much hardship in her life, and she didn't like being in the shelter, either. She was quiet for a moment and looked a little sad. But then she perked up and nudged my nose through the bars of our cages.

"I think every dog in here deserves a home, and we should celebrate whoever gets one," she said. "It doesn't matter who goes first, or last—every step forward is good for all of us. It's inspiring."

"Thank you," I said. "If this works out, I'm sure I'll think of you Bunnie, I'll miss you."

"You'd better!" she said, and we both laughed.

On the day of the introduction, I walked into the visiting room with Aunt Cheryl and saw a petite, blond, energetic woman with warm eyes standing opposite us. I slowly walked over to Grace, my potential foster mother, but before I reached her I turned and looked back at Aunt Cheryl, who was smiling at us. Her smile gave me the confidence I needed, and I walked the rest of the way to Grace, unafraid and with my head held high. She stood still for a moment looking deeply into my big brown eyes, then kneeled on the floor and gave me a long hug and kiss. I stood perfectly still while she hugged me. The room was completely silent. As soon as she started to pull away from me, I leaped up and gave her a nice, big, slobbery kiss on the cheek. Both the women broke out into laughter. I sure hoped that meant Grace liked me and my kiss!

We visited for a while, and Aunt Cheryl continued talking with the staff and Grace. I heard Aunt Cheryl say that I felt warm and that the veterinarian continued to take my temperature and give me medication. The infection had been terrible, and I had still not fully recovered from it, but there was a good chance that I would return to full health in the near future. Unfortunately, the medical staff had advised Aunt Cheryl not to take me to play outside while I was still recovering because I could overexert myself. I was disappointed that I would not be running free through the grass and feeling the warm sun on my back. But I knew that she and the medical staff were making the right decision by putting my health first.

Before she left, Grace and I sat down with a staff person. I wasn't paying too much attention to the conversation, but my ears immediately perked up when I heard Grace ask, "Is there anything I should be aware of in regards to her behavior?"

The shelter employee looked down at me pityingly. "During her time here we have noticed some aggression towards other dogs. I think she's really awesome, but she can be a little unpredictable around other dogs."

"Stop! I thought. Don't tell her that!" If only I could have ignored that German shepherd when I first came to the shelter. But there was nothing I could do to change the past—I could only hope for the best.

"Ok," Grace replied. "Thanks for telling me." I wasn't sure whether this meant she would foster me or not. I whined softly, feeling a little nervous.

For ten more minutes, Grace chatted with Cheryl and the shelter staff, with me by her side. Then she abruptly cut off the conversation.

"I want everyone to hear this," Grace said. I started shaking. "I've worked with all kinds of dogs like Maryland. I know it is sometimes hard to judge them fairly, particularly in a shelter environment, as it is very stressful for the animals. Many are frightened, lost, sick and unsure of their fate. But even in my very short interaction with her, I know that she is not truly aggressive. She has been nothing but sweet to me. Look at her now! She is just sitting next to the chair, soaking up all of the attention from Cheryl and me, one of the calmest dogs I have ever seen."

"I couldn't agree with you more," said Aunt Cheryl.

"I've decided to be Maryland's foster mom," said Grace.

Aunt Cheryl, with tears in her eyes, began hugging Grace. Overjoyed, I thumped my tail on the ground. Then they both turned their attention to me with hugs and kisses. A few minutes later they waved goodbye and Aunt Cheryl, as always, whispered to me that she would return to see me next week.

I had to stay at the shelter for just a little while longer, but already my spirits had soared. I couldn't wait for Grace, my foster mom, to take me home and to tell Bunnie my big news.

WEEK 6

The following Monday, Aunt Cheryl and I met with the chief veterinarian who had saved my life and discussed my medical condition with him. Aunt Cheryl kept her hand on my back as I sat on the exam table, and we both listened to the vet.

"Maryland's recovering very well," he said, after taking a look at my stitches.

"How long will she have to stay here at the shelter?" Aunt Cheryl asked. She was as eager for me to be reunited with Grace as I was.

The vet looked at me and smiled, but there was a little sadness in his smile.

"I know Maryland has a foster home now that she's eager to get to, but I'd like to keep her just a little bit longer, so we can make sure she's completely better. And, she still has a skin condition we need to address. I'd like to think we can release her later this week."

My heart sank—so many days away from Grace and her hugs and kisses.

"Will she be ready for the Fourth of July?" asked Aunt Cheryl. I didn't know what she meant.

"We'll try for it," said the vet, and though I didn't know what the Fourth of July meant, I was just happy to hear that soon I'd be at my new foster home. I didn't know what it would be like, but I was excited to find out!

Until then, I had dreams of what a foster home would be. At night, I saw visions of a cozy warm bed and a fireplace next to a window where I could watch rain and snow fall while I cuddled with my foster parent or doggie friend. I drooled at the thought of an endless supply of fresh water, food and healthy treats. I imagined myself running free in a huge yard filled with dozens of balls and large trees that provided shade in the summer. I tried to control my excitement when I woke up in those mornings after particularly vivid dreams, but the truth was that I wanted to feel it if only for a moment. I had never known this kind of excitement before. Now a foster home was not some distant illusion in the back of my mind, but an actual reality. As the week wore on, I was experiencing many new emotions. I was anxious and nervous, afraid that I would do something wrong and ruin my chances with Grace.

Throughout the week, Aunt Cheryl continued talking with the shelter veterinarian to arrange for my release to my new family. They detected a heart murmur, and I had a decayed tooth that would need to be extracted when I got stronger. My skin condition was getting better but had to be monitored. I was raw from fleas, but they did not yet know if there were other issues causing irritation, so they would monitor me closely. I didn't realize how sick I had been until I started to feel good. I didn't know anything different, so I thought that it was normal to feel tired, hungry, itchy and depressed all of the time.

Needless to say, it was the happiest moment of my life when I received the news that I would be released in time to go to my foster home for the Fourth of July weekend. The day I was scheduled to leave with Grace, the shelter staff gave me the spa treatment. They bathed me, cleaned my ears, brushed me and clipped my nails. Everyone at the shelter—even the ones who hadn't understood me because of my breed— pitched in to prepare me for my new home. It had been almost seven weeks since this phase of my journey began. I have to admit that I had mixed emotions, especially flashbacks to that day in May when I knew I had to take a chance. Today was another step in my long journey toward happiness. It was time for me to put my fears aside and be happy. The realization of my dream of a loving family was now a real possibility.

My foster mom, Grace, arrived at the shelter on July 1 as the doors opened at 10:00 a.m. The staff worked with her to complete my release papers. I feared that all of my medications might be too much for her, but she'd had foster dogs in the past that required more medication than I did. It was difficult to comprehend that I was finally getting my freedom to be a pet that can play and enjoy life instead of having to worry about my very survival. The shelter staff said their last goodbyes and there were even tears.

Thankfully, Aunt Cheryl had convinced the shelter staff and director not to give up on me and for that I am eternally grateful.

Before I left, I had to say some important goodbyes to my friends in the kennels.

"I'm going to miss you so much!" cried my little friend, Bunnie. "You deserve this."

"I'll miss you too," I said, nudging her through the bars of the cage with my paw. "It'll be your turn soon, I hope."

She sighed. "Maybe," she said. "But then again, maybe not—but whatever happens to me, I'm glad that I met you, Maryland. I've watched you become happier and also calmer around all of us other dogs. You've grown here though I know it wasn't all very fun."

I smiled and thanked her. I wanted to believe that what she said was true. I had tried so hard these last few weeks to overcome my past and to be the kind of good girl that a family would want.

Later that day, I met Grace in the front room of the shelter and immediately jumped up to give her a big wet kiss. I had decided that she liked them.

As I walked out of the shelter with Grace, I paused and looked back. I thought of the past few weeks and felt pain for all of the other animals who still longed to find loving homes. I remembered how at night I would hear whimpers and wonder if they longed for their families or if, like me, they were lonely and frightened. All of them dreamed of a kind touch, a safe place to sleep, and someone like Aunt Cheryl and Grace to love them. I wanted to do what I could to help them if I ever got the chance.

When we got into the car, Grace watched me as I took my place and sat like a lady in the passenger seat. I wanted to make a good first impression on my foster mom. My last memory of riding in a vehicle was the rescue van, and this experience was incredibly different— there was no cage, the seats were very soft and I could see out the window. I was enjoying watching my surroundings and was amazed at how much there was to see. Other cars passed us by while people strolled down the street, and dozens of houses with big green lawns popped in and out of view. For the first time in my life, I was experiencing the sensation of a breeze against my face that came through a rolled down car window.

At one point, two loud black vehicles passed us by. I would later learn that these were police cars and that the loud noise was from something called a siren. I would hide from sounds like these because my life on the streets had taught me that they could be a sign of looming danger. This time, however, I didn't hide or even flinch because I knew that I was safe with Grace. This drive was the first time where I could truly say that I had no fear of my surroundings. All of those new smells, sights and sounds were wonderful, but little did I know that the best was yet to come.

As we drove down the street to my new home, I noticed how different it looked from Maryland Street. The homes were newer with children outside playing; everything seemed inviting. We were now in a quiet western suburb of Detroit. As we pulled into the driveway, I thought that my new home was beautiful and a bit intimidating because of its size. However, the front yard looked small, and I was worried that there wouldn't be much room for me to play outside, which was one of the things I had looked forward to most. But, I would soon learn that I would play in a fenced backyard that was very large with lots of space to run.

The red brick two-story house looked gigantic once we walked up to the front steps of the large porch. At the top of the green front door was a small hanging photo of a black dog. What better entrance could a dog get? Still, I was not sure what to do because I'd never even been close to entering a home before. I thought of my friend Bunnie, and I wished she was here, she'd know what to do. After a slight pause, I entered the house.

Standing there in anticipation were two of my three adopted doggie brothers.

"This is Frankie," said Grace, petting the wrinkled head of a little male pug, "and this is Ozzy—the wild man!" Ozzy was a black and white boxer who looked very similar to me. His stubby tail wagged back and forth when he saw me.

"And you'll meet Marshmallow tomorrow—he's at the vet today," Grace said.

I was a little overwhelmed, but I kept my composure as Grace took off my leash, and I was free to say hello.

For a moment, we all stood and looked silently at one another.

"Boy, she's a little beat up, huh?" Frankie whispered to Ozzy, referring to the bald patches on my back.

"What do you mean?" I asked. I felt a little hurt but not threatened. I was determined to play it cool. After all, this was my new home, and I had to respect the fact that it might take them some time to get used to me, bald patches and all.

"Lay off, Frankie," said Ozzy. "Mom said that she's

had a hard life as we have. Be nice." He walked slowly up to me, and it wasn't long before all of us began to sniff each other. Then, like a true gentlemen welcoming a new guest, Ozzy licked my face!

Then Frankie said, "Aw, I was just kidding earlier, Maryland. Welcome to the family."

My foster mom knew that Aunt Cheryl was waiting anxiously for word on my homecoming, and I sat by my new mom's side as she sent an email:

Maryland has landed and meeting my motley crew was very uneventful. She was super sweet to my two dogs that are here. Ozzy loves her, and she likes tennis balls! She has not shown any aggression or dominance. She is just hanging out—goes outside to lie on the deck or hangs in the kitchen with me. Now relax and know that you saved a wonderful creature! She is in good hands, and we love her very much.

Aunt Cheryl sent out an e-mail to all of her friends who had donated to the Maryland Fund, as they were also waiting to hear how I was doing. That was the beginning of the first day of my new outlook on life! It truly was my independence day: Aunt Cheryl had given me the freedom to forget my time as a stray on the streets of Detroit. I welcomed being trained, eating at scheduled times and sleeping together in one big bed with my foster mom and brothers. After all, that was what family was about, and I was finally part of one. My first day in my foster home was truly a dream come true!

WEEK 7

As I settled into my new home, Ozzy became my closest friend. We curled up in the big bed together, and he told me more about my brothers and how they'd come to be with Grace. Like me, they had all been abandoned, taken to shelters or rescued. Ozzy had been born into a family of three boxer pups. All three of them had been dropped off at a shelter after their mother was killed by a car, and the owners would not take care of them. Ozzy was the only black and white dog that did not look like a boxer, so no one wanted him. Because he had pneumonia and worms, he needed extra medical attention. My foster mom adopted him when he was seven weeks old, and he'd been with her for eight years. Frankie the pug, the youngest and smallest of Grace's crew, was found on the streets of Ann Arbor and was brought to a shelter. He had a skin disease called mange and was dehydrated, but he recovered very quickly. He was about six months old when Grace adopted him. As Ozzy told me the story, Frankie snorted and pretended to be asleep.

"He's a little shy at first, but he likes to play ball," Ozzy whispered, "so next time we get to play outside, toss one around with him. He'll love you for it."

My first morning in my foster home was great: we ate, took care of our morning business and went on a walk. When we returned to the house, the three of us waited patiently for Grace to get dressed. She had turned on the television, which was a completely new contraction for me, and I learned that I was not the only dog celebrating her independence that week. As Grace turned the channel to the news, we all heard an exciting announcement:

"In other news, last night saw the end of a dog fighting ring that had its 'paws' in eight different states! During the raid, over 450 pit bulls, bulldogs, and more were rescued from this dog fighting syndicate, making this the largest bust in doggie history. And now, on to the weather…"

"Did you hear that?" I asked Ozzy. He smiled and nudged me in the shoulder.

"You bet I did," he said. "Today's a pretty great day!"

"I just hope all those dogs find good homes like you and I did," I said.

I again reflected on how fortunate I had been to be a rescue from the streets and not to have ended up being abused. If each of those dogs had the opportunity to recover from their pain and tell their stories like I now was, the impact may change people's mindsets and end dog fighting!

I didn't have too much time to think about my new furry friends because Grace suddenly led us out the front door and to the car. I thought, *Oh, good, a ride!* I had found one of the first of many delights as a pet.

Grace drove us to her business, a doggie day care center. I had no idea that such places existed, and I was jealous of all of the dogs who had gotten to spend time there because it was so much fun. Inside were dogs of all breeds and sizes to play with in addition to dozens of toys and bones. It was certainly what most canines would envision to be their heaven! After my trip there, my mom wrote to Aunt Cheryl:

I took Maryland to work with me today, and you have got to see her! She is amazing. Right now, she is in the gym playing with about twelve other dogs, and she is hilarious. She loves balls, and when she tries to stop to catch them, her back end keeps going. We all had a pleasant night yesterday. She slept in a king-sized bed, and we all cuddled together.

Later that night, I finally met the third of my new brothers, Marshmallow. Grace brought him home from the vet, where he had stayed overnight to have a small cyst removed from his side, and as soon as he walked in the door, I turned to say hello. He looked very similar to me, with short fur and a wide face, but he was pure, snow white. I had decided not to be shy. I wanted him to like me! But Marshmallow backed away and arched his neck, making it clear that he was not interested in saying hello. He looked me up and down and then grumbled, "Great, another stray. Save me the sob story, ok?" Then he walked over to his doggy bed, shaking his head.

"What did I do wrong?" I asked Ozzy. "You didn't do anything," he said. "Marsh is just a grump. He wishes he could be the only dog in the house. But don't worry. He warmed up to Frankie and me, and he'll warm up to you, too."

Then Ozzy filled me in about Marsh. Frankie and Ozzy were used to my foster mom bringing strange dogs home, as I was the twelfth foster dog, but Marshmallow was another story.

"We're all a little cautious when a new dog gets fostered here," he said. "You never know what they might have been through in their life. But Marsh...he's had a tough time, and he gets jealous of other dogs having Grace's attention. I think he might be a little scared of other dogs too."

"What happened to him?" I asked. I could certainly understand being nervous around other dogs after living on the streets, but Marshmallow didn't need to be afraid of me. I was a good dog who was just happy to be with Grace and the others.

"Marsh was taken to a shelter with his brother," Ozzy explained. "They were removed from a home because they were tied to a fence on a six-foot chain with no food or water. Marsh was skin and bones when he was first rescued." Ozzy described to me how Marshmallow had been separated from his brother at the shelter. The owner easily gave up the brother, but it was more difficult to convince him to let Marshmallow go to a new home. Marsh lived at the shelter until Grace was asked to foster him. Once Grace took him home, she worried that the owner might get him back, only to abuse him again. She put pressure on the shelter to encourage the owner to give up his legal rights to the dog, and when he finally agreed, Grace adopted him. Because of all that he had experienced, Marsh only truly felt safe with Grace and became, as Ozzy said, a little jealous of all the other dogs.

After talking with Ozzy, I knew that befriending

Marshmallow would be my greatest challenge. In my first weeks there I tried several different things to get to his heart. When he was hungry after a long session of playing fetch in the backyard, I would share some of my food with him. One afternoon, he was lying down after a big meal, and I walked over to him with a ball in my mouth to let him know I wanted to play. I dropped the ball in front of his nose, but he sent it rolling across the room with his paw, stood up, turned in a circle and laid back down with his tail against me. I felt crushed by this rejection, as I wanted nothing more than to be friends with him. I was sad about the way our relationship was starting out, but I was determined to keep trying to win him over.

Even though Marshmallow didn't warm up to me right away, it was still clear to Grace that the shelter workers' assessments of my behavior were nothing to cause worry. Grace had years of experience with dogs of my breed and their behavioral issues. One night, after another failed attempt to get Marsh to play ball with me, Grace scratched me behind my ears and gave me a loving pat on my back.

"Don't worry Maryland…he'll figure out what a sweetie you are, just like I did!" She sat down on the couch, and I curled up next to her so she could continue petting me. "I sensed right away that you weren't a hostile dog," she said. "A lot of people don't realize that the way a dog or cat acts in a shelter isn't always the way they'll act once they're someplace where they feel safe and loved. A shelter is a stressful place for a dog like you, isn't that right?"

She was right. I had been very frightened and nervous in the shelter, always on my guard. The other dogs there were frightened, too, which made us all a little wary of each other. But if I'd learned anything there, it was that we acted out because we were desperate to be loved and taken care of in a real home.

As the days flew by, I was getting more and more comfortable with my new mom, brothers, and surroundings. I was also very curious about the neighborhood and eager to explore. Grace's was so different from Maryland Street! One trick I liked to do in those first few days at Grace's was to open doors. I was great at it! One day, I nudged open the sliding glass door and started sniffing around to learn a little more about this part of the city. Grace took me out on a leash all the time, so I figured it would be okay to go outside by myself. The only thing between me and the sidewalk was Grace's fence. As I stood there, trying to figure out my next move, I heard the other dogs in the doorway behind me.

"What does she think she's doing?" said Frankie. "She can't jump that."

"Maybe you can't," laughed Oz. Marshmallow was sitting with them, but he didn't make a sound. Instead, he just watched me curiously.

"She'll never make it!" barked Frankie.

"Wanna bet?" I said, feeling playful. I stepped back to get a running start and then jumped! I grabbed the top of the fence with my paws and scrambled over. I was outside the yard on the sidewalk where smells of other dogs wafted around me. On the other side of the fence, I could hear Ozzy and Frankie laughing and cheering.

I was ready to explore. I spent the afternoon walking the same route Grace usually took me. I stopped here and there to sniff at a tree trunk or to look for dogs that I had seen before on walks in case they wanted to play. Eventually, I found a nice big tree, a lot like the one I used to lie under on Maryland Street, and from there I surveyed my surroundings. Everything here was so clean and nice, with gardens in each yard and a beautiful park to play in. I felt lucky that Grace had chosen to bring me here.

As the afternoon wore on, though, I wondered whether Grace and my brothers might be worried about me. After all, Ozzy, Frankie, and Marshmallow hadn't followed me on my adventure. I suddenly became nervous that maybe I wasn't supposed to wander around. Anxious, I started to make my way back home.

The problem with living in a new place, though, is that the scents just aren't as familiar. I had trouble following my trail and all the houses suddenly seemed to look alike. I was lost!

I wandered around on the sidewalk as the sun started to go down, and I felt even more nervous than before. What if I never found my way home? Would Grace be sad if I never came home? Would the other dogs miss me? I didn't want to get picked up by another man in a van and taken to a shelter again. I just had to find Grace!

A couple walking a small white Shih Tzu dog came down the sidewalk in my direction.

"Do you know Grace? Or Ozzy or Frankie or Marsh?" I called to the Shih Tzu.

The dog pulled on her leash and hopped back and forth. The couple led her across the street, away from me.

"Never heard of them!" yipped the little dog as her family whisked her away.

I felt hopeless. Finally, I had found a place I wanted to call home, but I didn't even know how to find it! As I padded forlornly down the sidewalk, I saw people looking at me from their windows and yards. It was just like Maryland Street again. They seemed afraid of me. I missed Grace.

"Maryland!"

I heard Grace's voice just then, calling my name. My ears perked up and I tried to figure out from where the sound was coming.

"Maryland, come here, girl!"

Then I saw her holding my leash and standing at the corner. I bounded over, so happy to see her that I jumped up and tried to give her a kiss.

"There you are!" she said, as she clipped the leash to my collar. "You scared me…you're not supposed to go outside without me." She knelt down and scratched my head. Her eyes were sad, and her forehead creased with worry.

"Part of having a home is staying there and being part of a family…you don't wander off!" I had never thought of it that way before, and I was sorry that I had made her worry about me.

She took me home, and I decided that was plenty of adventure for me. From then on, I would be a good girl and stay close to home.

On Monday, Grace took me with her to doggie daycare and from there she wrote Aunt Cheryl to tell her about my adventure.

We had a little scare over the holiday weekend with our girl, Maryland. It seems that she is very smart and clever! We found out that she can open doors—sliding glass doors, metal doors, doors with knobs, and doors without knobs! Just now at the day care, she just held the back door of our outside area open for several dogs to come inside—it was the cutest thing. She is very cordial, but an escape artist. On Saturday, she was at the daycare with me until 1:00 p.m. then I brought her home and shut the house up and turned on the air conditioner. Though my sliding glass door was closed, it was not locked. She opened the door, got over the fence (part of it is six ft. and the other is four ft.) and took a stroll through the neighborhood! Everyone said she was looking for me because she is so attached. She is home safe and sound, but I was a wreck! I have a trainer and a new lock for my door.

Later she sent Aunt Cheryl another note:

She is great, a real love. She sleeps with me every night, but usually gets hot and moves to the couch. She loves to go for walks and is never too far from my side. All in all she is a perfect foster. Ozzy is madly in love with her, but she plays hard to get!

All was well, and I felt something I never felt before: that I could trust Grace, and that she could trust me.

WEEK 8

After a full week at Grace's, I was so happy that I couldn't even imagine having to leave. Grace took me for a walk twice every day and let me play in the neighborhood park. Nothing like the park had existed on Maryland Street. I loved rolling around in the green grass and running through the wide-open space. The most exciting thing about going to the park, though it sometimes made me a little nervous, was the chance to meet some of the neighborhood dogs. During my first few trips there, I could tell that Grace was nervous, too. She held my leash very tightly to keep me from jumping and scolded me when I barked hello to a pair of Jack Russell terriers. The other dog owners looked at me with concern when I walked by and tried to say hello to their dogs. I knew that, even though this neighborhood was nicer than Maryland Street, I'd still face the same uneasiness from the humans around me until they got to know me better.

Grace more than made up for my anxiety with treats, ear scratching and belly rubbing at home. At night, I curled up with her and my brothers in one big bed which put my failed attempts at neighbor dog companionship right out of my mind. Things were definitely getting better for me. After ten days in the house, even Marsh was starting to be friendly. He even said "good morning" to me one day!

All this time, I was getting attention from people

outside my new foster family as well. Aunt Cheryl and Grace spent time updating their friends who had donated to the Maryland Fund on my progress, and their encouraging words were overwhelming:

Amazing! I thought the shelter said Maryland was not good with other dogs? But, it appears she is very good with other dogs. That will help her for adoption. Honestly, I think you should adopt her...I wonder if anyone can love her as much as you do.

I suggest we have a Maryland Fan Club! It is so nice to see how the two of you changed her life around so completely in such a short period. Also, a tribute to her that she's able to put her past behind her and do so well.

I can't tell you how happy I am that things turned out the way they have! "It takes a village" apparently applies to rescuing dogs too! She looks wonderful, and I'm pleased to see that she's happy with other dogs. She's a lucky girl!

It made me feel so special and loved knowing that so many cared about me and believed in me. I was grateful for all of the effort that Aunt Cheryl had put in to ensure that I would have a second chance.

In mid-July, Aunt Cheryl came to visit. I was very excited, as I had not seen her for over two weeks. I couldn't wait for her to meet my foster family! When I heard the doorbell ring, my brothers and I ran to the door barking. I heard her voice as she walked in.

"Hi there, baby," she said, and I jumped up to greet the woman who had saved my life. My tail wagged furiously in excitement. She knelt down, hugged and kissed me, and asked me to sit. I did, and she pulled out the chewy treats I loved!

Both her and my foster mom marveled at how smart I was. We all moved outside on the deck so Aunt Cheryl could watch me interact with my foster mom and three brothers. She saw how protective I was of all of them, especially Grace and Ozzy. When the boys started playing rough, I was the new sheriff in town. Leave it to me to keep things cool! I sat by her feet while she petted me, and when I looked into her eyes I saw her happiness. As she petted me, she looked me over and smiled.

"You're such a gorgeous gal, Maryland!" Grace laughed. "Let's call her GG for short…Gorgeous Gal!"

I wagged my tail and turned in a little circle. I loved it. I did feel like a gorgeous gal! I was thrilled that Aunt Cheryl was proud of me. I was GG!

Aunt Cheryl and my foster mom talked, laughed, and cried about all of the rescued animals they had encountered over the years. I was interested in hearing about one of Aunt Cheryl's kitties, Carlton, who had recently become quite famous in the community. He was very personable, meeting with schoolchildren at events and "speaking" to reporters! I heard them remark that my experience was one of the greatest and most interesting stories they'd ever heard (besides Carlton's, of course). At one point, Grace told Cheryl how special I was and how much she loved having me in her home. Aunt Cheryl whispered to her, "Well, my secret hope is that you'll adopt Maryland."

That was my secret, too. Maybe, I thought, if Aunt

Cheryl and I hoped hard enough, I'd have a chance to stay with Grace, and she would love me forever. Cheryl and Grace sat on the deck discussing my medical conditions while I played in the yard with Frankie and Ozzie. I heard them say that my tooth needed to come out. Oh no, not another surgery! The last one had been so frightening.

"It's all so expensive," said Grace. "GG's medical bills were already over $1,500 even before the tooth surgery. Of course, it's worth the money for her to be healthy."

Cheryl put her hand on Grace's shoulder. "That's exactly why groups like the Maryland Fund are so important," she said. "By working together, we can make a difference. People all over Detroit care about rescuing dogs like GG, and we have come together to help. The Fund raised over $2,000 dollars…it should cover all of it."

Grace smiled again.

"It's amazing, isn't it?" she said. "Sometimes you see these dogs and you wonder how you can make a difference for so many. But we can!"

I was amazed, too, as I listened. Only a few weeks ago, I had felt all alone in the world like no one would ever notice me, let alone help me. But to hear Grace and Aunt Cheryl talk about all the people who cared enough about me to help, I was overwhelmed. If Aunt Cheryl had not worked so hard to raise the money to care for me, my fate might have been different.

They visited a while longer and then Aunt Cheryl

stood up from her chair. She hugged and kissed me and then, with sadness in both of our eyes, I walked her to her car and sat at Grace's side. As they stood saying goodbye in the driveway, though, Aunt Cheryl's voice took on a sadder tone.

"It is amazing what we've managed to do for GG," she began, "but not everyone can see it. I was in a meeting at one of the shelters recently talking about her rescue, and I asked for donations to the Maryland Fund. Nearly everyone offered to help with whatever they could afford whether it was $1.00 or $100. But, as I was talking, an employee of the shelter rolled her eyes and said 'There are thousands like her. Are you going to save them all?' I was shocked and very hurt, but I said, 'Yes, I'll sure try. We can save this one and make a difference in her life, and we'll save others too, one at a time.' "

"That's exactly right!" said Grace. "People need to see that these dogs are such wonderful companions. Each dog and cat are worth saving. We must try. And, is that not what shelters are there to do? To save the lives of all healthy and treatable animals who enter their doors?"

"That's why I hope more people can meet GG," said Aunt Cheryl. "She's a special gal. When people get to know her better, they'll see why we need to save as many of these wonderful animals as we can."

Aunt Cheryl and Grace hugged, and I sat at Grace's side as we watched Aunt Cheryl drive away. I was saddened by Aunt Cheryl's story because it made me think about all of the animals I'd left behind in the shelter. If everyone thought like the woman who rolled her eyes, what would happen to them? But I liked what they had said about me. If more people got to know me, then maybe I could make a positive difference like Aunt Cheryl, Grace and the ladies who had contributed to the Maryland Fund. I wanted to try.

A few days later I got more bittersweet news, a reminder that Grace's home was not my permanent home. Grace came home from work, walked and fed me and the boys, and then picked up the phone. I stopped eating my food as I heard her say, "Hello, Cheryl? It's Grace." I listened with my ears perked.

"I received an email from a pit bull rescue yesterday." Grace said. "Someone is interested in adopting our GG."

Oh no! I thought. In the shelter, I had wanted nothing more than a forever home, but now that I had begun living with Grace and my brothers, I never wanted to leave. What could I do?

"Yep, I did get some information." I heard Grace say. "They mentioned that she has another dog, a cat and a two-year-old child. That's all I know."

I could hear Aunt Cheryl's voice faintly coming through on the phone. She sounded excited and happy, but I was miserable at the thought of leaving. My heart thumped in my chest.

"You're right, I should call her today," said Grace. "This is pretty exciting!" But her voice trailed off in question.

No! Don't call her! I thought. I'm perfectly happy here! I waited on edge as Grace dialed the woman's phone number. As the ringer buzzed softly, my heart sank and Ozzy and Frankie padded over to sit with me. They sensed something was going on.

"So. Good news," said Frankie.

Ozzy, however, hung his head.

"But I don't want to leave," I said. "I want to stay here with you."

"It's hard every time a foster leaves," said Ozzy. "We'll miss you, too. You've become a part of our family."

That's when I heard Marshmallow approach from behind us.

"How are you with cats?" he asked me gruffly.

Cats, I'd never dealt with cats before. The stray ones on Maryland Street had pretty much stayed away from dogs like me.

"I'm not sure," I said. "Why?"

"Grace said the woman had a cat. Just something to think about." With that, he walked away to be alone on his doggy bed.

Grace began leaving a message on the phone.

"Hi, you were interested in meeting Maryland. I'm the one fostering her. Give me a call and we'll set up a time for you two to meet. She's a very special dog!"

I hoped that the woman wouldn't call back, even though I knew I ought to be grateful.

A couple days later, I was lounging with my brothers in the backyard while Grace did dishes inside. Marshmallow lay on the grass a few feet away from where Ozzy, Frankie and I were catching some sun. Suddenly, all four of us perked up our ears. We smelled something! I looked over to the corner of the yard where there was a small opening in the fence between the neighbor's house and Grace's. Sure enough, there was the neighbor's cat, a yellow striped kitty named Sassafrass, moseying into our yard. I had learned that if you ignored Sassafrass, she left you alone, but she did walk around like she owned the place. I was ready to lay my head back down when I realized what Marsh had been saying in the kitchen the day Grace had called the woman about my adoption. I could decide here and now to show Grace that the woman's house wouldn't be a good fit for me. It would take a little bit of an act, but if I wanted to stay, I had to do it.

I made sure that Grace was watching from the backdoor window and got up to chase Sassafrass. I immediately started barking and the cat's back arched. We had never challenged her before. I made a little promise to myself to apologize the next time I saw her. I ran full tilt to her, and she dashed up a tree, hissed and cried, "What are you doing?" I jumped at the base of the tree, barking and yelping.

"GG! Down!" Grace hurried out the back door and ran over to me. I didn't want to play too rough, after all, I knew that if Grace thought that I couldn't behave, she might not want me around, cats or no cats. I stopped jumping and walked over to Grace, as I growled one last time at Sassafrass for good measure.

"I've never seen you run like that!" Grace exclaimed. I realized, with relief, that she was laughing. "That's not nice, GG," she continued. Her laugh died, but she was still smiling a little bit as she scolded me. "You have to be nice. Don't chase kitties! That's a no!" I knew that I had been naughty, and I didn't want Grace to worry. But as the days passed, and no visit with the woman on the phone was ever arranged, I felt relieved and a little giddy. If it worked, I thought to myself, I'd never misbehave again, ever!

Soon after that, Grace and Aunt Cheryl talked again. On the phone, Grace told Aunt Cheryl that I wasn't ready for adoption yet. My heart almost stopped, as I wasn't sure what she meant.

"I think GG needs a little more time here with me," Grace said. "She's a good girl, but she still has some things to learn. Maybe we should take her picture down from the adoption site…just for now."

I felt all sorts of emotions. I was sorry that I had let Grace down, but I was so happy to hear that I wouldn't have to say goodbye yet! But I wasn't sure how Grace felt about me now that is until she sent Aunt Cheryl the following message:

I cannot thank you enough for coming over to visit. The pack enjoyed their bones and treats very much! Maryland remembered you, and Ozzy was so happy to meet you. Ozzy even got in your purse for your keys to keep you from leaving! He wanted you to stay! I believe that people and dogs come into our lives for a reason as well. It has been my true pleasure to become friends with such a compassionate and caring animal lover! You amaze me! Every one of my dogs has taught me life lessons. For instance, Taz taught me to be slow and detailed. Ozzy taught me to let loose sometimes. Sydney taught me to love even when I don't want to! Frankie teaches me to smile every day. Marshmallow taught me to look for the light at the end of the tunnel.

What may you ask has Maryland taught me? Well, until today I did not know for sure. But today I found out! When I feed the dogs, I put all the dry food in their bowls and set them on the kitchen counter. I then go to the fridge to get the canned food to add to the dry. Tonight, Maryland decided not to wait for the canned food. She simply hopped up on the counter, picked up her bowl, walked it to the rug in front of the fireplace, sat it down, and started eating!

I was amazed. She did not spill a crumb, did not falter, and enjoyed her dinner on her terms! Well, since she has been with me I've been struggling with my business, both financially and emotionally. It is draining and stressful and nothing would be easier than to give it up! But then I look at Maryland. She could have given up, but she didn't. She pushed on with what little she had left to give. She is a survivor! Anyone can give up, but it takes someone very special to push forward in the face of difficulty. Thanks to Maryland, I will do just that! When we talk about saving animals' lives, we may just want to turn that phrase around. In so many ways, they save ours. Thank you for bringing her to me.

WEEK 9

My tooth removal was on July 28, and I was very scared. After all, my last surgery had been very difficult, and I had developed a life-threatening infection. In addition to this, I learned that I had an irregular heartbeat, also known as a heart murmur. We did not know how bad it was, but because I would be unconscious for the surgery, the veterinarian would need to be extremely cautious. I was nervous, but I understood that the surgery had to happen. My tooth had gotten badly decayed and could cause other problems if it were not removed. It was also starting to hurt a little bit.

Asleep on the operating table, I had a very vivid dream about my puppies. In it I was curled up with all of them, comforting them as people came to take them away to good homes. When I woke up, I felt relieved about my puppies and realized that my mom was petting me. She soothed me by saying that the surgery had gone well and that there were no complications. I was still a little sore and very woozy, but I was the healthiest I had ever been in my entire life. Even my skin condition had healed from the oatmeal bath Grace gave me. We discovered it was due to stress and bad diet.

Grace took me home and put me in a special doggy bed in her room. I was still groggy from the surgery and needed plenty of rest.

That night, I was surprised when Marshmallow was the first one of my brothers to come and check on me. "Hi there," he said as he settled down on the floor next to

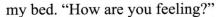

my bed. "How are you feeling?"

"Ok," I said, finally feeling a little more alert. "Just glad the last of these visits is over."

"For now," Marsh said. "There's always another visit to the vet to look forward to…" We both laughed, and then Marsh was quiet for a minute. He was the friendliest he'd ever been to me. I wondered what was bothering him.

"I just wanted to tell you that you've been brave," he said. "A lot of dogs that come here, they're scared because of what they've experienced. I should know, I'm a lot like that myself, but I'm impressed with how much you've become a part of our family."

"Wow, thank you, Marsh," I said. It was the nicest compliment I'd ever gotten…except maybe when Aunt Cheryl called me a gorgeous gal!

That night, we both had trouble falling asleep, and he described to me what his life was like before Grace found him.

"Maryland, it is still hard for me to think about my life before this. There are many days that I am still hurt and angry. But I want you to know the truth."

"Ok, I'm listening," I told him.

"I had an owner before Grace. But he didn't take care of me. He kept me tied up to a fence for what seemed like years. I didn't have any food or water. The only time I had water was when it rained. I didn't have anything to keep me warm during the harsh winters or cool during the hot summers."

"How did you feel that whole time?" I asked gently,

thinking about my friend the Chihuahua and how she'd spoken so kindly to me.

He paused. "I was always depressed, always lonely." I heard the pain in his voice. "I even thought it was my fault, and I didn't understand why that was happening to me."

"It wasn't your fault, Marsh," I assured him.

"I know that now. But what he took away from me was my ability to trust. Humans, dogs, other animals, I don't like anyone to get too close to me."

I smiled to myself in the dark. "That's ok, Marsh. You don't have to let everybody in your life. I understand that. When I lived as a stray in Detroit, not a single person reached out to me to help until Aunt Cheryl. My first owners took my puppies away from me. I understand it is difficult to trust again, but we must try."

"I guess we do have a lot in common, don't we, sis?"

"I think we do," I said.

After that, we started sleeping beside each other. One night, I cautiously decided to lick his ears before bed. At first, he appeared to be annoyed with me, but I soon discovered that he loved it! But my biggest accomplishment was getting him to play with me. As I began to truly understand and become acquainted with Marshmallow, I knew that I couldn't have asked for a better canine companion.

My relationship with Frankie was also improving. After my adventure over the fence, he was almost protective of me. We played tug-of-war with rope in the backyard, and after I let him win a few times, he loved me almost as much as Ozzy did. The four of us became inseparable.

It was the love of Grace and the companionship of my brothers that made me feel completely safe for the first time in my life. My brothers and I shared a connection because we were all rescues, and we were bonding as siblings. We played, shared, got into mischief, and even had little squabbles, but we were a family and nothing could change that…unless I was adopted by someone else.

My mom continued to send Aunt Cheryl updates, and she passed them on to her friends:

Maryland is doing very well. She loves life and is one smart cookie. She is a good dog, and if I am not at the law firm, she is with me. She is extremely attached and is never more than 2 feet from me when we are together. She likes to sleep on the couch after a long walk in the morning, so if I am not at the daycare, she is at home. No more escapes.

When she is on a leash, she gets excited if she sees another dog! Once she is with the other dog, though, she is fine. She is great with all the dogs she has met, big and small. She listens well and knows her name. All in all, she is a pleasure, and we all love her very much.

I was so happy that my foster mom was patient with me, understood my behavior, and was willing to work with me. I truly believed that I had been given this second chance to help change people's views of my breed and of all shelter animals.

WEEK 10

One morning, Grace announced that we would be attending a special breakfast at a fancy hotel in Birmingham, Michigan. She said we would make our debut with bells on…whatever that meant! The event was for the shelter that I had stayed at when I was rescued. Then Grace told me the strangest part of all: I would be one of the featured guests! I would be introduced in front of a large room full of people who were interested in my rescue. Grace said that this was because of my breed.

"You're going to show them what a good girl you are, GG!" Grace said. I was proud that I could help others. The day I'd been taken away from Maryland Street had forever altered the course of my life. I was eager to share my story and I hoped it would change the lives of thousands of other animals.

The day before the event, my mom took me to the spa for a bath and bought me a new pretty pink collar and leash. I was ready for my debut and anxious to find out what it meant! We got up very early the next day because we had to be at the hotel by 8:00 a.m. As Grace packed some treats for me, I saw Marshmallow watching us get ready from the bedroom door.

"I wish you could come with us," I said. Behind him, Ozzy and Frankie were still sleeping.

"And have to trot around in front of all those fancy people?" Marsh said. "Not a chance!"

I shook my head, laughing a little. I should have known that Marsh wouldn't have anything nice to say.

"But you have fun, ok, GG?" he said. I was surprised. I gave him a hesitant lick on the ear and rushed off to meet Grace.

We arrived in a wealthy suburb of Detroit. From the car window, I could see all sorts of tall buildings and expensive brick homes. My mom parked the car and, as we walked toward the hotel, I smelled hundreds of purple flowers. Two men stood in front of the hotel's wide glass doors. I was very worried that they might ask me to leave once they saw me. But instead, they smiled and even opened the doors for us. When we walked in, I felt like a pampered princess…a gorgeous gal!

We found ourselves in the grand lobby and immediately I looked all around, wanting to take it all in. The floors were slick, shining marble. Overhead, a crystal chandelier glistened and the room was full of velvet furniture, large paintings and vases of fresh flowers. We walked up a short flight of stairs to a very large hall where dozens of people in suits and dresses stood around talking. My foster mom and I weaved through the crowd and suddenly I heard Aunt Cheryl's voice. I gently pulled Grace towards her.

"Hi there, baby," Aunt Cheryl said when she saw me. She knelt down and gave me a big kiss. I was so happy to see her in this strange and wonderful place. I wagged my tail so much that I almost lost control of my whole rear end. She and Grace had a good laugh at that. Soon after we'd arrived, one of the staff came over to our group.

"We just wanted to let you know, Cheryl, that another rescue dog, Coco, is here." The lady said. "So you might just want to keep an eye on Maryland. Thanks!"

Cheryl thanked the woman and then turned to Grace. "When are we going to be done with this 'aggressive' nonsense?" she said. "GG's the sweetest dog I know."

"She'll be just fine," said Grace, ruffling the fur between my ears.

As for me, I wondered if the other dog was in a foster home or was lucky enough to have gotten adopted. I was sure I'd find out before the breakfast was over. And if I got the chance to meet Coco, then I'd have another opportunity to prove to people that they were wrong about me. I wanted them to look beyond the stereotypes that they had been taught to associate with my breed and see me for the loving dog I truly was. I knew that I would be proving this negative perception wrong my whole life, but in doing so I would help the next generation of dogs like me, just as Bunnie had said!

As Grace and Aunt Cheryl continued to talk about other rescue dogs they knew, I heard them describe my Chihuahua friend at the shelter. To my surprise, Cheryl told Grace that she had recently been adopted by a wonderful family who had two other Chihuahuas. My heart filled with joy for Bunnie and I wanted to tell her how happy I was and wish her all the best with her new family. But, it got better, much better! The Labrador puppies found a loving foster home. And, Cleo's puppies were rescued from the horrific dog fighting ring, along with 12 other dogs. She was now back with her puppies; they were all safe. My heart was full: it was a wonderful day!

When it was time to enter the main dining room, I found myself in the presence of four hundred people and felt like a princess all over again. We walked up to the front of the room and sat at a table near the stage with Aunt Cheryl and some of her friends who had donated to the Maryland Fund. I was introduced to everyone and many people came over to meet me. Aunt Cheryl brought me my favorite treats. I sat down between my mom and her as waiters brought out plates of eggs, bacon, toast, pancakes, waffles, coffee and tea. The breakfast looked so good, but I knew not to jump up and I sat patiently on all fours like a lady. The waiter brought me a big bowl of fresh, cold water. At one point, my mom and Aunt Cheryl snuck me a few morsels of table food. I was so proud of myself because I had not begged for it. They gave it to me for being so good.

Finally, breakfast ended and the program began. There were many rescue stories like mine and sadly many dogs were badly abused at the hands of their owners. Some had collars embedded into their necks. Others were starved and beaten. But these dogs, like me, had been lucky enough to get a new beginning.

Towards the middle of the program, I saw a tall, slender man with graying hair take the stage. Although he tried to smile, it was obvious that he was about to disclose some very painful information to the audience. He cleared his throat and began to speak.

"Seven months ago, I was working at the shelter when a brown and white dog walked through the door.

Coco, as we named her, had been rescued from a place which must have seemed more like hell than a home. The signs of her abuse showed that she had been beaten for many years. She had been kicked and pushed by her cruel owners who had broken some of her ribs. When the owners decided to leave Detroit, they left Coco tied up to their back fence with no food, water or shelter. In the dead of winter, this poor dog was rescued. Half dead from starvation, dehydration and frostbite, many of us at the shelter did not believe she could be saved. Amazingly, after several weeks of intensive treatment and love at the shelter, the worst was over for her." I saw tears glisten in the man's eyes as he introduced Coco. She looked a lot like me: white fur with brown spots. She even looked just as happy and healthy as I felt.

Aunt Cheryl was the last person to speak, introduced by Alicia of WXYZ TV News in Detroit. As she walked up on the stage, I saw that she took my treats with her and I wondered why.

"Thank you, Alicia," she said. "Don't worry, everybody. These treats aren't on the menu." The crowd broke out in laughter.

"Good morning, everyone. Thank you for coming out this morning for this very important event. Today I will be sharing with you the story of a very special dog named Maryland, we call her GG, Gorgeous Gal!"

My ears perked up. I knew Aunt Cheryl was telling the story through my eyes. She began with, "My name is Maryland," and then began telling my story. The audience was so engrossed that you could hear a pin drop. At one point, I noticed she had tears in her eyes. Soon the whole room of people had tears in their eyes, too.

When she finished telling my story, she closed with "Love, Maryland" and then asked Grace and me to come up on stage. She introduced us, kissed and hugged me, and gave me a treat. Everyone applauded for the two of us and I felt incredibly special and fortunate. Never in a million years could I have imagined that this day, this amazing day, would be part of my incredible journey.

Lastly, Aunt Cheryl told the crowd that she was the one who had rescued me on May 20. She talked about how much I had touched her life and thanked the shelter staff and all of her friends who had believed in me and had donated to the Maryland Fund.

"We are their voices, so let's speak loudly for them! Together, we can make a difference as we did for

Maryland and Coco!"

When she finished and thanked the audience, there was thunderous applause. After the closing remarks, so many people came up to my mom, Aunt Cheryl and me. Everyone wanted to meet me, the dog from Maryland Street, who just ten weeks ago had been scared, hungry and sick. After seeing Aunt Cheryl's passion for telling my story, I knew that she would continue to share it and that someday it would make a difference in the lives of animals and people all over the world.

Coco, I later found out, had been adopted. My Aunt Cheryl was receiving frequent updates from her mom. Coco was sweet and content in her home with her brother and sister, who were also rescue dogs.

WEEKS 11 - 13

Summer was slowly fading away, and I could feel the crisp cool air on my fur in the evenings when my mom and I went on walks. I also noticed that the leaves on the trees were beginning to change to colors of red and gold. When I lived on the streets, this change meant that I had to find good shelter before the first freeze and snow hit. Finding warm shelter was the difference between life and death for me in the winter season. This year I didn't have to worry; I could just lie on the deck and appreciate the beauty of the trees' changing colors. I knew that every night when the sun set I would be sleeping in a warm bed with my new family.

It was at this time that Grace brought some new dogs into the mix. I'll never forget the day Grace brought them home to be fostered: three short-haired terrier pups with black, brindled fur. They were only seven weeks old and they didn't know where their mom was. They'd been found huddled together in the corner of a parking garage in downtown Detroit. The moment I saw them, my heart went out to them. After a few days with the puppies in the house, Grace wrote to Aunt Cheryl:

I am fostering three puppies right now that are seven weeks old and "GG" could not be a better mom to them. She loves them, watches over them, and keeps them out of trouble. She is a natural mother, and I bet she misses her own babies very much! I have a video of her playing with the puppies, and she is so sweet and gentle with them. They call her mom! I could not ask for a better dog. "GG" showed up like she has always lived here and fits right in. She is never a problem, is very smart, and is mostly a couch potato. You saved an incredible dog. Thank you so much.

Not only was I happy to help Grace take care of the three newcomers, but I felt my energy and love for life renewed every time I played with the pit bull pups or cleaned their soft ears. Most nights I would cuddle up with them, licking their black fur until they fell asleep. During the day, I made sure that they ate well and stayed safe while they were playing. Although they reminded me of my puppies that I'd never see again, I felt that having them in my life was a blessing. I could finally pay forward the love that I had received from my brothers, Aunt Cheryl, and my mom to some very deserving little pups. Just as I had always wanted to do for my puppies. Finally, I felt at peace!

WEEK 14

One morning in early fall, Aunt Cheryl stopped to visit Grace and me. She petted me, put on my collar and leash, and led me to the backseat of Grace's car. They both got in, and Grace drove. It was the first time I had ridden in the car with the two of them, and it was exciting. As we passed through the neighborhood, the two of them talked. I didn't pay much attention because I was too interested in watching out the window as the houses passed by. After a while, my foster mom pulled up to a big brick house and parked the car. Aunt Cheryl opened the door to the backseat, held onto my leash, and led me up to the wooden front door. My foster mom followed behind us. I was suddenly scared. Where were they taking me?

I had been so distracted lately with the terrier puppies that I had forgotten that I, too, was still up for adoption. Was this the end of my time with Grace?

Aunt Cheryl knocked on the door and when it opened there was a short lady holding a tiny baby boy. I studied my foster mom to get a sense of what this visit with these strangers was about and I noticed she was smiling.

The lady was grinning, too. I waited on the porch until they both went inside. I then followed them into a room where a little boy and girl were sitting on a sofa. As soon as they saw me, they ran over and began to pet me. I have always liked kids and I enjoyed the attention, but it wasn't enough to calm my nerves. In the back of my mind I couldn't help but wonder if Aunt Cheryl and my foster mom were going to leave me. Was this my new family? I didn't want to leave Grace, so I ran over to her side and sat next to her. She took me by the leash and all of us went outside into the backyard, where Aunt Cheryl threw a ball. I ran after it and brought it back. She handed the ball to the little boy who threw it over the grass. I ran to get it and brought it back to him. He petted me and laughed. I was having fun but was too nervous to enjoy myself.

I looked over to Grace and saw her engaged in a serious conversation with Aunt Cheryl. They called me over to them and I was all too happy to sit at their sides. My leash flapped behind me as I sprinted towards them. Aunt Cheryl grabbed it, and I followed her and Grace through the backyard gate and back to the car. I'd had a nice time with the family, especially playing with the little kids, but I was very worried. After all I'd been through, I knew that my home was with Grace.

WEEK 15

As the long summer days were turning to the shorter and nippier fall evenings, Marshmallow and I had developed a routine that we both enjoyed. Every afternoon we would spend a couple of hours playing with tennis balls, my favorite, and running together in the backyard. After we had worn ourselves out, with our tongues drooping out of our mouths as proof, we would come inside to drink water and eat a delicious dinner. Once we had stuffed ourselves, we would curl up together in the living room on top of pillows and blankets that we had claimed for ourselves. I told him about the strange visit with the family of kids and he was very sympathetic.

"Lots of dogs come and go through here, but I'd feel pretty lost without you," he said. "You're my only sister!"

"What can I do to make sure Grace keeps me?" I asked. "This isn't like the time I chased Sassafrass…this was much more serious." A terrible thought occurred to me. "Maybe Grace is in a hurry to get me adopted. Maybe she doesn't want me anymore."

"Are you kidding?" said Marsh. "Grace loves you. We all do. If she finds a family for you, then you know it's going to be a good one because Grace only wants what's best for you. That's what foster moms do. She'd never adopt you to a family that you wouldn't love just as much as you love us."

"That's impossible," I said, nudging Marsh's head

with my own. "I don't think I could ever love a family more."

Marsh and I had shared almost every significant experience with one another since he'd opened up to me after my tooth surgery, with the notable exception of the breakfast banquet I had attended at the hotel. That's why I was completely overjoyed when my foster mom told me that Marshmallow and I would be attending a march for animals in downtown Detroit with her. She explained that it was a charity fundraiser event for local animal shelters and that I would again have the honor of being introduced, this time to thousands of people and their dogs, and even a few cats. This march would raise money for shelters across the Detroit region so that more animal lives could be saved. The biggest difference between the event and the banquet, though, was that we both would be marching with lots and lots of other dogs.

"I know you can do it!" Grace said.

On the morning of the march it was cold, and a mist of rain was in the air. The three of us loaded up in the car and drove the twenty-five miles from our home to downtown Detroit. We arrived around 8:30 a.m. and I could not believe what I saw! There were dogs everywhere: dogs of every breed and size, dogs dressed up in costumes, dogs in wagons, dogs in buggies, dogs in knapsacks lining the plaza to begin to march.

Soon after we arrived, Aunt Cheryl found us and said hello. She'd brought her famous cat, Carlton, but didn't think it was a good idea for us to meet just yet

gorgeous gal

considering the Sassafrass incident! She pointed over to where Carlton was getting ready to be on live TV!

"He's pretty brave coming down here with all these dogs," I said to Marsh. "I'd like to go on TV…well, maybe someday!"

"Count me out," said Marshmallow, scratching at his harness. "I'm already on attention overload."

The crowd kept getting bigger, and I noticed that, much like the dogs that had gathered there, people of all different backgrounds had gathered to support this noble cause.

Aunt Cheryl returned to Carlton, and together they walked onto a stage that had been set up in the plaza. She welcomed the crowd, introduced Carlton, and then waved to Grace. To my surprise, Grace led Marshmallow and me up on the stage!

"This is Maryland, Marshmallow, and Grace," Aunt Cheryl said. "Grace is Marshmallow's mom and Maryland is a recent rescue. When I found her, she was in poor health and wouldn't survive another summer on the streets. Just look at her now!"

The crowd broke into deafening applause! I wagged my tail and smiled, loving the attention. I could sense the pride of both Grace and Aunt Cheryl in me.

The event was starting, and I couldn't walk with Aunt Cheryl and her cat, so Grace, her friend, Marshmallow, and I began marching together. The misty rain had stopped, but it was still cold and damp. At one point, I was sure I saw my Chihuahua friend from the shelter. My heart skipped a beat in anticipation, but it turned out not to be her. I knew she had a home now, and this thought warmed my heart. Regardless of the weather, the dogs and their owners carried on, and Carlton as well, in his cozy warm stroller. I think he may have been one of only two brave cats at the march. All of the dogs were on their best behavior and were respectful. I was having the time of my life, but I think Marsh would have rather been home in bed. He was so tired that I often had to nudge him to keep him going. Despite the bad weather and exhaustion after our sixty-minute walk, we both took pride in the fact that we were marching to raise money for a local shelter. This money would help rescue, care for and adopt more animals like us.

This successful event was another incredible step in my journey. It was so heartwarming to see the thousands of caring people with their beloved pets marching along the Detroit riverfront. It was a reminder that if enough people are willing to care about and commit to a cause, positive change can happen.

WEEK 16

A week later, Grace heard back from the family she and Aunt Cheryl had taken me to meet. They would not be able to adopt me because the little boy was allergic to me. I pretended to be sad, but inside I was very relieved. I kept hoping that Grace would stop trying to find another family for me and would adopt me herself. I made an effort to continue to be well-behaved, patient and loving. I played nicely with my brothers and the three puppies, was calm when I met new friends on my daily walks in the neighborhood park, and no longer got into mischief. I wouldn't even glance twice in the direction of a cat!

"GG" The Princess

WEEKS 17 - 20

It was not too long after the march that Grace said that Marshmallow and I would be attending another event with Aunt Cheryl, this time for senior citizens.

"You're becoming quite the spokes dog, GG!" Grace joked.

I loved that...I wanted to help Aunt Cheryl any way that I could. I was excited that Marsh and I would be able to share yet another experience. He and I were developing quite the social calendar.

On the day of the senior citizens' luncheon, Marshmallow was very nervous. Grace drove us to the center, and when we walked in, Marsh seemed surprised to see a dining room of seventy people. He stayed close to Grace's side. But I immediately started making the rounds of visiting each table. I loved the attention and stopped for anyone who wanted to pet me. After visiting a couple of tables, though, I returned to Marsh's side.

"You like this kind of thing?" he asked me.

"Everyone here is rooting for us," I said. "No one's going to hurt you here—they're happy to see you."

Marsh let his tail droop, and he stopped looking around anxiously. But he still wasn't entirely convinced.

"I'd be much happier if it were nap time," he joked. We soon spotted Aunt Cheryl sitting with Carlton the Cat at a table in the back of the room. My ears perked up. I was eager to meet Carlton and to show everyone how good I could be around cats. I rushed to them as fast as I could. When I finally stopped less than two feet from him, the two of us locked eyes. Suddenly he stuck his front paw out and very gently placed it on my black cheek. I opened my mouth, panting playfully, and suddenly I felt tiny little pricks on my face where his paw was. His way of greeting me, but I never knew cats had little claws! I had a new respect for Sassafrass, and was relieved I didn't catch her!

This was a big test, and I knew it. I didn't whimper, pull away or retaliate.

"Oh, you have claws?" I asked instead.

"Meow," was his response.

I backed away proudly.

We had finally become acquainted! I was honored that my mom had decided I was finally ready to meet him. I could see how much Aunt Cheryl and Carlton loved each other. I also learned that Carlton had two brothers Big Boy, and Caesar and two sisters, Cissy and Chanel, all rescues. I thought, Wow, that's a lot of cats!

Marshmallow was watching me, smiling.

"Nicely done," he said.

Cheryl, Marshmallow, Grace, and I walked the room to greet the rest of the guests. Many of them lived at the senior center and didn't get to see pets very often anymore. My head received so many kind pats it felt a little tingly! But we hadn't gotten very far when I was stopped in my tracks by a woman who appeared nervous and was pointing insistently at Marsh and me.

"Aren't they pit bulls?" she asked. She looked at Aunt Cheryl with worry and held her hands up like she didn't want to touch us.

"There's no such breed as the pit bull," said Aunt Cheryl kindly.

"They're Staffordshire Terrier and an American bulldog mix," said Grace.

"There are a couple of those dogs in my neighborhood that are always barking," said the lady.

"They look ferocious."

"Well, dogs do bark," laughed Aunt Cheryl.

"I suppose so," said the woman, who looked down at Marsh and me. She walked away, without as much as a pat.

My feelings were hurt as this lady had chosen to focus on our breed as if that was all that she needed to know before making up her mind about us. I so wanted to do something that would help change her mind, but I wasn't sure what that could be.

During lunch, Marshmallow and I played a game to see which one of us could go the longest without begging for 'people food.' We were getting pretty good at it, but Grace always ended the game by giving us a little bit of bread, pie—even vegetables—to munch on. Marsh chomped happily on a piece of carrot while I sampled some pumpkin pie. It was clear to me that Marshmallow had overcome his shyness.

After lunch, Aunt Cheryl went up to the podium to finish setting up for her presentation. I was feeling restless, so I walked up onto the stage to see what she was doing. It was then that I smelled all sorts of delicious food coming from the nearby kitchen door. I trotted over and nudged the door open with my nose. The wait staff stood emptying the lunch plates over a few large trash cans, chatting with each other. But when they saw me, they went quiet.

"Oh gosh, look at that pit bull!" said one girl, backing away.

"Um…" Another server hummed, looking around for help.

I started to back away too, ashamed that I'd scared them, and sad that they didn't look at me the way Grace and Aunt Cheryl did. But then Aunt Cheryl appeared by my side in the doorway.

"Hi guys, this is GG," she said. "She was rescued from Maryland Street in Detroit in May, and she's a sweetheart."

She told them a little more about me and about how misunderstood pit bulls are. One by one, the wait staff stepped forward, and each petted me on the head and neck.

"She is good," said the girl who'd backed away from me earlier. I licked her hand. I was so happy to have heard her say that.

One young waiter came up to me and spent quite a long time petting my back. When he stopped, I started licking his hand.

"You're such a sweet dog, GG," he said. I thought I'd burst with pride.

Finally, it was time for Aunt Cheryl's presentation. She talked about animals like me who had no homes, and she said that it was humans' responsibility to care for them. She said that people needed to have compassion and respect for their pets as well as a desire to care for all animals.

Towards the end of the speech, she told the story of my rescue and recovery. I watched the pain and sadness in the faces of the audience turn to joy when they learned about my foster mom, Grace.

As Aunt Cheryl spoke, I walked around the room and spotted a serving tray on a small table. I suddenly smelled pumpkin pie. Tempted by the sweet aroma I was about to grab the leftover dessert, but I heard her say softly from across the room, "No GG." I was obedient and left it alone. The ladies chuckled. I normally had better manners than that, but it was worth a try, especially for something so tasty.

As she finished her presentation, Aunt Cheryl reminded the audience of some of the many things that I had learned after my rescue. Adopt from local shelters and rescue groups, provide proper medical care, and speak out on behalf of abused and voiceless animals. She then closed with the following quote:

"The greatness of a nation and its moral progress can be judged by the way its animals are treated."
-Mahatma Gandhi

I felt that this was an excellent quote to end the luncheon. If people were willing to let stereotypes impact their treatment of dogs, then this could certainly be the case with groups of people, as Grace had taught me. The ladies at our table came to say goodbye to Marshmallow and me. They commented that because of us they had learned how lovable and friendly pit bulls can be. The woman who had been pointing at us earlier stopped by our table. She was an older woman dressed in gray pants and a blue blouse. She looked very sad.

"Hello," she said. "I just wanted to apologize to the both of you for what I said about your dogs earlier. Your presentation was inspiring, as were the stories of these truly remarkable furry friends."

"That's why I do this work," Aunt Cheryl said with a smile.

"I guess I never thought much about how the stereotypes associated with them could lead to more abuse and neglect," she said.

"Many people don't," Aunt Cheryl replied. "But we are glad that there is one more person in the world who knows today."

I smiled. These were exactly the seeds that all of us had been hoping to plant in hearts and minds.

This successful event gave me a great sense of pride and joy. We had changed the view of seventy people today, and if we could change it for them, we could change it for seventy more and seventy more, one day at a time.

gorgeous gal

Marshmallow and I now slept regularly on the couch together, and sometimes he would lick my face to show his affection. I smiled inside because I knew he was beginning to love me.

The next big event of my life was quickly approaching, Halloween. I had no idea what this was, and I was definitely in for a big surprise. My foster mom was very creative and loved to make clothes for dressing us up. She had learned the hard way in years past that Ozzy and Frankie are not into costumes, but Marshmallow and I were happy to dress up and go trick-or-treating together. I was a Princess for Halloween and Marsh was Dracula. Grace explained to us the story of Dracula, and even though Marsh is all white, I must say he made a good one. I didn't look too shabby myself with a pink hat that had my initials "GG" on it and a pink tutu. Unfortunately, we were not allowed to eat any candy, but the neighborhood children loved us, and we had fun seeing the hundreds of different costumes out there. I was officially a Princess! Mom gave Aunt Cheryl an update after this milestone:

I thought it was about time I sent out an update and some pictures of Maryland. I know that you and all of her friends are curious about what she is up to these days. Maryland (aka "GG") spends most of her days going to the park, playing with friends, and just loving life. As you will see from the pictures below, she went trick-or-treating as a princess and looks excellent in pink, her signature color! She was so happy and well-behaved at the breakfast last month. I was very proud of her.

WEEKS 26 - 27

The winter holidays were quickly approaching, and I hoped that my dream of spending Christmas morning with my permanent family would come true. I was still afraid that Grace would decide not to keep me and give me to a new family. But I also knew that I had come very far since the day of my rescue in May.

This week was the Thanksgiving holiday, and I certainly was very thankful for my life today. There were so many people who had touched my life, and I only hoped that they knew how grateful I was. I no longer dwelled on my past, but I would never forget it. I was not angry with anyone for abandoning me or bitter that no one in the Detroit neighborhood had befriended me when I needed them most. Instead, I focused on the fact that my past experiences had made me stronger, more loving and more compassionate. I was certainly grateful for my loving foster mom, brothers and safe home. But I was even more thankful that I now had the opportunity to do work on behalf of other neglected and abused animals.

Thanksgiving Day was very busy. It started with my usual morning walk, but not with my foster mom. She volunteers at a local animal shelter and regardless of the occasion or weather, she faithfully walks homeless dogs. So, while she went to walk the dogs, I was visited by her friends Molly and Jeri. I met Jeri's two rescue dogs, Kia and Salsa. I greatly enjoyed making new friends and these two were such fun. Kia is a Shiba Inu. She looks like a little fox, has a wonderful personality and loves attention. Salsa is a seven pound Chihuahua but he thinks he's a Great Dane! Seeing him made me think about my Chihuahua friend in the shelter, especially since they had similar personalities. I thought of Bunnie often and was so happy she had found a family to love her. We all went out to the park for our walk and, of course, I kept an eye on my guests. I guess it's my maternal instincts, but I love to watch over my family, friends, and all of the foster dogs Grace brings home.

When we got home from the park, Jeri made sure to tell Grace how good I had been with Kia and Salsa. "It's hard to believe the shelter said she was aggressive," she said. "She's as sweet as they come."

"I know," said Grace. "I like to think that we help that happen by giving them love, but I think deep down, they're all like that at heart. With a little trust, even the most nervous dog is a sweetheart. I'm so glad she has been able to leave those days behind her."

I was glad, too. My brothers, Kia, Salsa and I all took a nap while Grace, Molly and Jeri started cooking Thanksgiving dinner. I love my long naps but as the aroma came out of the kitchen I slept with one ear on alert waiting for the dinner bell to ring. Food never smelled so good, and I sure hoped I'd be lucky enough to get some morsels. I was ready for my first Thanksgiving dinner with my family—actually, my first Thanksgiving dinner ever.

My brothers, guests and I had mashed potatoes and stuffing along with our regular food and we also got some pumpkin pie for dessert! I remembered the pumpkin pie from our recent luncheon, and it was just as tasty as I had imagined it would be. After our big dinner, my foster mom took me for a short walk.

Then we all settled in to watch movies and cuddle by the fire. I loved the fireplace, and I loved cuddling, too! My foster home was just like I'd hoped it would be back in the shelter. I wished I could tell Grace how grateful I was for making me a part of her family, but I knew that I didn't have to because she could tell every time she looked into my eyes.

WEEKS 28 - 29

gorgeous gal

The next few weeks were very busy. My foster mom was bringing in dozens of packages, and she put a tree up in the house. I thought that having a tree in the house was odd, and I was pretty sure it was not a good alternative to the ones outside.

"What are you doing?" asked Ozzy when he caught me sniffing all around the tree excitedly.

"Trying to figure out why this tree is so special and gets to come inside," I said. "Do we get to use it?"

"Huh?" asked Ozzy.

"You know…" I squatted a little to show him what I meant.

"Oh! No, no, we don't do that," he laughed. I laughed too. "It's a Christmas tree," he continued. "It's a human thing—not totally sure what it means, but just wait until Grace gets done decorating it. It'll be the most beautiful thing you've ever seen."

When Grace played Christmas carols and trimmed the branches, I quickly learned that the decorations on it were not for my amusement. Another lesson learned.

I couldn't wait for Christmas Day to come! I had dreamt about it for so long, it was hard to believe that it was only a few weeks away. As it got closer, I became more and more interested in the everyday activities so that I could get a better understanding of the meaning of Christmas. I wondered if Maggie, my old friend from Maryland Street, was right and if I would receive extra love and treats on that day.

I soon found out that Christmas was not only about presents and material things. About a week before Christmas, Aunt Cheryl came over for a special dinner. In the spirit of the season, she told us a heartwarming story. At her office, they have a giving tree to help neighborhood families who are going through tough times. One family had a mom, a son and a dog named Lucky. The son asked for Santa to bring Lucky milk bones and chew toys, but he didn't ask for anything for himself.

"That is real love!" Aunt Cheryl said. She and her husband bought Lucky a ten-pound box of milk bones, two chew toys, a Christmas stocking and a gift card. In the card she wrote that Lucky was very fortunate to have them as his family. Aunt Cheryl said that the boy's unselfish deed was in the true spirit of Christmas!

After dinner, Aunt Cheryl said she had a surprise for us. She gave Grace a gift card to a local pet store for my brothers and me. Later, Grace helped us all write her a thank you note in a cheery red and green Christmas card:

We can't thank you enough for your very thoughtful and generous gift. We all talked about what we wanted for Christmas, and we remembered when all we hoped for was shelter, food, and water. Today we were making a wish list for Santa! Ozzy wants bones and soft toys; Frankie wants bones, peanut butter cookies, and a new blue sweater; Marshmallow wants bones, and no more dogs in the house besides Maryland; Maryland (GG) wants bones and peanut butter filled cookies. GG will sure have a great "first" Christmas thanks to you. We love you!

WEEK 30

Just a couple of days before Christmas, I heard Grace and Aunt Cheryl talking on the phone for hours. They hadn't talked this much since Grace had decided to foster me. I didn't know whether it was a good or bad sign. I spent the whole day fretfully gnawing on a dental bone, watching Grace as she walked from room to room. Finally, I turned to Marshmallow.

"What's going on with Grace?" I asked him, interrupting his afternoon nap. "Why is she talking to Aunt Cheryl so much today?"

Marsh gave me a knowing look and smiled.

"Not a clue," he said—but his grin told me something else.

"You do know!" I said, nudging him. "You have to tell me! I'm going crazy worrying!"

"I have no idea, sis," he replied, yawning. "But I think you can probably relax."

Now I was more anxious than ever. I spent a very sleepless night wondering about Grace's strange behavior. By morning, I was determined to get to the bottom of it. When I got up, Grace was sitting in front of her desk, as usual. When I put my paw on her knee, she smiled broadly and waggled my ears.

"Guess what?" she asked. "I'm writing a note to Cheryl to find out where I can sign to adopt you."

Now Marsh's smile made sense. I was overjoyed! Finally, after many weeks, I was going to have a real home. Grace finished her email to Aunt Cheryl:

GG has made our family complete, and we love her very much. I cannot imagine my life without her.

I was so very happy. I couldn't imagine my life without my family, either.

Aunt Cheryl announced my adoption to the Maryland Fund group of women:

I am thrilled to announce that Maryland's dream came true and she has found her permanent home. She has been adopted by Grace, her foster mom. Grace is a wonderful lady and we could not ask for a better, more loving home for "GG." She is spoiled, sleeps in bed, has a beautiful yard, and goes for daily walks. These last few months have been a labor of love, and it could not have happened without the generosity, compassion, and support of each and every one of you. I want to thank each of you from the bottom of my heart for believing in Maryland and me, to help her get a second chance. Of course, I also want to thank Grace because without her compassion and generosity, Maryland would not yet have her permanent home.

My Mom—my Mom, I love saying that!—read me the comments from Aunt Cheryl's friends:

That brought tears to my eyes. I have been there and done that, and I completely understand the feeling when you find a loving animal a permanent home. There is nothing more wonderful.

Maryland is an awesome dog, and she deserves the very best. You gave her that! Without you, she would have died on the streets never having shown others what a great dog she is.

How precious! I just love her. I'm so happy you adopted her...you are the best! Thanks so much for sharing! She's blossomed into a gorgeous girl thanks to you saving her and Grace's obvious love for her!

What a wonderful story! That brings tears to my eyes. Yeah for you and GG! I continue to be amazed at her transformation! Thank you for sharing.

I had just one last thing to say to Aunt Cheryl: Thank you! I knew of no other way to express my gratitude to her for giving me freedom and allowing me to take this wonderful new journey in my life! I hoped she knew that I tried my best to prove that she was right for believing in me.

As Christmas drew closer, Grace introduced a new houseguest, a seven-week-old white lab mix named Chilly.

"Too many dogs in this house already!" Marsh grumbled, but he couldn't hide how much he loved Chilly. She cuddled up to both of us at night, and again I couldn't help but think about my puppies. If I could make Chilly feel safe and loved, it was like I was doing the same for them. I always dreaded the day when our foster dogs left us to go to their new homes. But I also knew that we were helping them through tough times. Grace's fostering gave them a chance to find wonderful permanent homes. But I would always have good memories of dogs like Chilly and the puppies who came to stay for a little while. I hoped that, like Grace, I was helping them, too.

On Christmas Eve, we went for an early walk so that we would not miss Santa in case he stopped by early. When we returned, we ate a special dinner with my favorite treats and mashed potatoes mixed with my regular food. Afterward we all snuggled up by the fireplace for our long wait for Santa. I was so excited I could not sleep. My eyes were heavy, but every time I dozed off I'd awaken. I knew he would not come until I was asleep, but I didn't want to miss anything. My heart filled with excitement and I couldn't wait for Christmas Day, the first day that I would celebrate being part of a family, a family that loved me.

The next morning, I woke up to the sound of Grace calling us all into the living room to see what Santa had left us. Marsh, Ozzy, Frankie, and I ran from our bed, our toe nails skittering on the floor.

Underneath the tree, I found all kinds of presents: healthy white bones, tug toys and a beautiful silver crown all for me! I was a spoiled princess, after all.

Chilly, our white lab foster puppy, was excited, too. I grabbed a treat in my mouth and plopped it onto the floor in front of her.

"Merry Christmas, Chilly," I said. "Maybe by next year, you'll have a forever family, too."

Chilly nuzzled my nose and rolled over, and we all laughed. My heart felt very full.

After Marsh, Oz, and Frankie had opened their presents, we all sat together in front of the fireplace. We looked out the window watching the beautiful snowflakes glisten as they softly floated through the air and settled quietly on the ground. I remembered my conversation with Maggie about Christmas, and I became overcome with gratitude for both of us. We'd found families at last. I made a Christmas wish that all of the dogs and animals who lived out there on Maryland Street and beyond, who were lost, frightened, sick and lonely, would find happiness like this. It would take a long time. But if enough people were willing to give them a chance, then they could all be as loved as I felt right now, looking out the window at the blanket of snow with my very best friends. *Oh, Maggie, I thought, it is even better than you said it would be. It is truly a magical time of year. I am home, finally home.* I nuzzled Marsh and lovingly licked Grace's hand. My journey, at long last, was complete.

"GG" Ms. Personality

IN MEMORY OF GG

Rescued May 20, 2009 -
November 4, 2014
(Age 10)

GG was the "greatest" dog! She was my inspiration for *GG's Journey*. She has also been my inspiration to help save homeless animals, both great and small, and provide humane education to youth and adults. I rescued her in May 2009 in Detroit, Michigan on Maryland Street. We were told by the shelter that she was aggressive and unpredictable...and she proved herself to be NEITHER...she was the MOST loving and gentle dog! *GG's Journey* depicts the challenges faced by many dogs on the streets, due, in great part, to the stereotypes associated with pit bull breeds. Beginning with surviving the streets of Detroit, and nearly dying from peritonitis resulting from spay surgery, GG was a survivor, and she never gave up. We are not certain of her age at the time of her rescue. She may have been four or five. In the fall of 2009, Renee (Grace) adopted GG...a joyous day that I will never forget!

In April 2014, GG was diagnosed with anemia and they found a mass on her liver. She had a great summer, but her health began failing, and she was hospitalized on November 3, 2014, for anemia and dehydration. On November 4, 2014, I said my goodbyes to GG and she crossed Rainbow Bridge.

Renee (Grace) was the best Mom ever and gave GG the most wonderful life, full of love and adventure. Thankfully, she allowed me to remain a part of GG's life. We will go on in GG's spirit to help other animals, she would have wanted that. GG, you gave us so much love and joy! I love you, GG and I will miss you! You were a truly beautiful, gentle GG...a Gorgeous Gal to the end!

(Below is a letter penned by GG's mother, expressing to me what she knew GG would have said when the time came near for her to ascend the Rainbow Bridge…)

"Dear Aunt Cheryl,

I will never forget the day we met. I just knew from the look in your eyes that you were my Guardian Angel sent to help me live the life I was meant to live. No other person looked at me with such love and care. No other person took the time to see my loneliness and suffering. Because of you, I became a dog with a name, a dog to be loved, and a dog with a home.

Saying goodbye to you was so sad, but know that because you helped me, I lived my last years with fun, walks, an abundance of love and food...I was someone's GG. Thank you for giving me a home and thank you for helping me reach the Rainbow Bridge. We will meet again, but know I am now your Guardian Angel. Each time you help another animal, when you look in their eyes, you'll see mine dance. If you need a friend, one will be there. You're never alone, and will never be forgotten.

My gratitude and love for you lives on.
Love,
GG"

GG'S FAMILY

Ozzy passed away in 2014. He spent 13 years loving and playing with all the foster doggies that Renee brought home. He was the foster greeter and he made sure each dog felt at home. He particularly loved GG as she was an easy going, fun gal to hang with. Marshmallow spent every day loving life and smiling. He would wake every morning and tell us a story. He would talk and bark and I never saw a dog so excited to start his day. He loved to fetch the ball and would run for hours keeping Ozzy at bay. Marshmallow died of mass cell tumor cancer in 2013. Frankie is a Pug with a big attitude. Because he lived with Ozzy, Marsh and GG he knows what it is like to be a big dog! Frankie misses his big doggie family, but now lives with Dudley and Ivy – both pugs. He is enjoying being the "alpha dog" for once.

ACKNOWLEDGMENTS

There are so many people and animals who have been sources of inspiration, support and encouragement to me. First, I thank God for giving me the courage and stamina to rescue animals, give them a voice, and the inspiration to write GG's story through GG's eyes.

My Husband, Patrick

My Mom, Virginia, for her prayers

Carlton, my Ghostwriter, who sat by my side on a pile of papers hour after hour while I wrote

Caesar, Cissy, Chanel and Big Boy, my loving felines

Renee (Grace), GG's Mom, my dear friend

Carol, who read and re-read copy after copy

Franco, Grazie for believing

Jane Schwyn, educator and dear friend

My dear friends Melonie, Nancy and Darlene for their support

Morgan and Brooke

Christina LaRose, Editor, who encouraged me, a novice writer, and believed in GG's story and without whom this book would not be where it is today

Allison LaRose, Editor, encouraged me to write from my heart, and edited copy after copy

Cate Fricke, Editorial Specialist

Deidre Stierle, Graphic Artist, cover design

Kim Hinman, Greko Printing Graphic Designer, cover design

ABOUT THE AUTHOR

Ms. Phillips developed her love and respect for animals at a very early age when she tended animals at her great-grandparents' dairy farm in Rochester, Michigan. She formerly served on the board of directors for the Michigan Humane Society as Secretary and chaired the Humane Education and Marketing and Development programs. Cheryl also chaired the Detroit Public Television Be Humane program. She has volunteered for the Humane Society of Huron Valley where she assisted with the rescue of animals and TNR (trap, neuter, return) to prevent animal homelessness and overpopulation. Cheryl is involved with protection activities to speak on behalf of our furry friends for humane treatment of animals and humane education for people, animals and the planet.

Cheryl Phillips has held the positions of Vice President, Masco Corporation Foundation and Director of Global Purchasing for Masco Corporation. She holds a Bachelor of Science in business from Madonna University and an MBA from Eastern Michigan University. Cheryl is an adjunct professor at the University of Michigan-Dearborn. Her awards include the Twilight Benefit Civic Leadership Award (2014), YWCA Western Wayne County's Women of Achievement Award in the category of Dedicated Volunteer (2007), and Distinguished Volunteer by the National Society of Fundraising Executives (2003).

Ms. Phillips lives in Northville, Michigan, with her husband and their three feline fur babies. GG's Journey is Cheryl's first novel.

AUTHOR'S NOTE

I was inspired to write this book, through GG's eyes, to bring awareness to the plight of pit bulls and all abandoned, homeless, neglected, and abused animals. It is through this writing that I hope to instill an awareness of the often subjective "temperament testing" resulting in the classification of animals that may deem them unadoptable. These classifications can ultimately lead to their death at the very hands of those entrusted to protect them. The ASPCA (American Society for the Prevention of Cruelty to Animals) estimates approximately 7.6 million companion animals enter animal shelters across the United States each year, and each year, 2.7 million animals are euthanized! What can we do to prevent overpopulation, abuse, and neglect? Spay or neuter our pets, volunteer at the local shelter, or become a foster.

All companion animals deserve a chance to live a life filled with love and compassion. Please do not abandon a pet, they are not disposable! If you cannot keep or care for your pet, please take your pet to a reputable animal rescue or shelter. Give your pet a chance to find a loving family. Humane education is a critical component in helping our animals and eliminating abuse and neglect. In July 2015, I rescued a 12-week old kitten. He was being fed cereal, and the woman said she got him because cats "do not" need care like dogs…he had a terrible case of parasites. Jasper is now healthy and living in a loving home with his sister, a Saint Bernard.

"Educating the mind without educating the heart is no education at all." Aristotle

May God Bless and watch over our animals.